7.95

THE
CONCENTRIC
PERSPECTIVE

WHAT'S IN IT FROM ME?

ERIC
BUTTERWORTH

Unity Books
Unity Village, MO 64065

TABLE OF CONTENTS

INTRODUCTION

The Concentric Perspective deals with a fundamental process in human existence that is rarely considered in the study of metaphysics. This process is both simple and profound. But if you can really grasp the idea, it will lend a whole new dimension to your awareness of your relationship to the universe and to your practice of Truth.

Normally a course of study is introduced by defining terms and communicating notebooks of information. However, in most cases I don't like definitions. I believe, like the Orientals, that to define a thing is to limit it. I want to give emphasis, not just to "in-formation," but to the "out-formation" of certain depth potentials within.

Educators often use the word *pedagogy*—the art of teaching. A pedagogue is a teacher of children. The word comes from two Greek words meaning "child" and "to lead." At one time the pedagogue was the slave who accompanied the child to and from school. So pedagogy is simply leading the child toward learning. As a teacher of Truth I am expected to be a pedagogue. However, I am more concerned with what I call "auto-pedagogy," the art of self-teaching, self-direction. I set for you, the student, the goal of becoming your own guru, of taking yourself by the hand and leading yourself forth on the quest.

We sometimes call ourselves Truth seekers. But the truth is that there is no need for seeking. We must first learn not to seek "out there," for when we seek there is a tendency to go window-shopping, and thus to achieve a consciousness that is a patchwork of metaphysical slogans. Truth is within—not something to search for, but something to awaken to and release. Truth is at the center of you, the mystical point where God becomes you, a point of changeless oneness. You *exist*, which means "stand forth." You are the activity of God expressing or pressing out into visibility *as* you.

If you are to progress as a student, it is important to get rid of old frames of reference. If you insist on holding to old perceptions, the old anthropomorphic concept of God will all too often rear its head. It is to this center of truth within you that Jesus refers when He says, "Go into your room and shut the door" (Mt. 6:6). To experience a balanced life and an attitude of confidence and courage, it is important to continually return to the center, to deal with life *concentrically*.

We will be using this word frequently throughout the book. You may have used the word *concentric* in reference to circles or spheres, one within another, all having a common center. Imagine, if you will, an ever-widening series of circles emanating from you at the center. Note that wherever you are or whatever you may be involved in, you can never get outside the circle of which you are the center. The key to effectiveness, or the solution to conflicts, is to return to the center, which interestingly defines the word *concentration*.

From the concentric perspective, concentration is not focusing on something outside, but rather on becoming the focus for the expression of something from within. This reveals why a centering time of meditation is the key to the prayer for help in solving problems. When, like the prodigal son, you are out in the far country of a broad circle of human experience, you must come to yourself and arise and go unto the Father, so that you may return to your center of oneness with God.

Of course, we are referring to God, not as the great Being of the skies to whom you appeal for help, but as omnipresent or "omni-centered." This center within you is God at the point of you. At the root of you, the ground of your being, you are *Being* being you. You are the "self-livingness" of God. In a more real sense, you are the "self-givingness" of God. The highest objective of human experience should always be to give way to life.

ONE

DISCOVER THE WONDER OF GIVING

The starting point of a spiritual study is usually God. One begins with definitions and inexorably builds a theological structure. But it is all on the outside, an intellectual construct, and one is reduced to looking in the window. All religions and their divisions and schisms begin in this same process.

We want to begin from an entirely different perspective. We want to commence with *you*. So, for the moment, let go the thought of God as something extraneous to you. Say to yourself, "I exist!" Think about the physical you. Whatever it is, it *is*! It is fresh; it is sensual; it is beautiful. Through the senses we become aware of our environment. Unless we see from the perspective of "I exist!" we tend to look out into our environment as if we are insignificant nothings in the vastness of the world "out there." From this sense of insufficiency we make such statements as, "Isn't God wonderful?" and "Isn't nature grand?" Of course they are, but the point is, *you* are wonderful and grand and beautiful. We are concerned here with how great *you* are! This is our starting point.

You live in an environment you do not see. You see things, but you probably do not see reality. Can a fish see water? Can a person see God? You are environed by God; you live, move, and have being in God. God is all, the universe. And the universe is centered at the point where you are as the "eachness" of your transcendent self.

Before you go any farther with this chapter, take some time to reflect on this idea. You are the focus of an infinite idea. You exist! So, you are Being being you. If you are good at visualization, imagine this symbol (or you may want to draw it on the margin of this page): two cones laid out horizontally, touching at the points. This is formed by drawing two straight intersecting lines. In the left cone print in large, bold letters, "BEING"; and in the right cone print in smaller letters, "being *me*."

Now reflect upon three ideas: There is a mystical center in us all; the whole of God is present at every point in space; God is the environment and the center in which I live, move, and have being. You are the center—that point within you where you are God as the ground of your being. Get back to this point of Oneness within . . . often.

In the ensuing chapters, we will be dealing with Truth and with you *concentrically*. We will keep reminding you to get back to the center and to deal with Truth as a flowing forth out of this center. At the root of you, at this point of Oneness, you are Being being you. Actually at this cosmic center you are Being. You are whole all the time, not just when you are speaking words of Truth. The need is to concentrate often on this center, which Paul calls "Christ in you, the hope of glory" (Col. 1:27).

The study of Truth often awakens in the student the desire to become spiritual. But you are spiritual! Spiritual growth entails concentrating, not on becoming something, but on Being. An acorn doesn't concentrate on becoming an oak tree; it is an oak tree. Its natural concentration is in being. Thus, it naturally unfolds the power to split asunder any boulder that would obstruct its growth.

Get it established in consciousness right at the outset that what you are seeking is seeking you. It is in you. The whole universe is breaking through to you. God is Being being you. Let go the tendency to try to achieve Oneness. You are one. Let go trying to achieve healing. You are whole.

In the hit musical *Zorba*, there was a marvelous scene in which, to the music of Greek instruments and with dancing and rhythmic clapping, the question is being asked over and over again: "What is life?" And many interesting answers are given. Undoubtedly you have asked the question at some time in your life, possibly out of desperation, or when your back has been against the wall, or when some great injustice has happened to you: "What is life? What's it all about, anyway?"

Life cannot be defined. If you try to come up with an adequate definition, you simply end up with a lot of meaningless words. Life can only be lived from within-outward. When you catch the idea of living from within, you realize that life is a giving process; you discover the wonder of giving. "For God so loved the world that he gave..." (Jn. 3:16). All life, all love, all substance, all wisdom flow forth from within.

For many persons it is a veritable quantum leap to a new concept of the "omniaction" of God and of the spiritual potential within every person. It is probably true that many simply jump into the new practice without rightly identifying it as the law of our being. No doubt the most difficult step in "getting" the message of Truth is unlearning a lifetime's conditioning to the idea of God "up there" to whom we must go on bended knee, begging for His mercy. The Truth is that God is an ever-available all-sufficiency which we experience as we consciously "give way" to the divine flow.

Erich Fromm, in his *Art of Loving*, gives an important new meaning to giving: "For the productive character, giving has an entirely different meaning. Giving is the highest expression of potency . . . This experience of heightened vitality and potency fills me with joy. I experience myself as overflowing, spending, alive, hence as joyous. Giving is more joyous than receiving, not because it is a deprivation, but because in the act of giving lies the expression of my aliveness."

In the last few decades there has been an amazing change in the life-styles of people of the Western world due to the impact of some much-discussed revolutions. The feminist movement has succeeded in achieving new freedom at home and at work. Computers and robotics have invaded the marketplace and changed our lives. Sexual attitudes have grown more relaxed in description and in practice. Minority groups have steadily moved up into the middle class. But there is another marked change that has gone virtually unnoticed. It is the attitude toward money and success and the acceptable methods of achievement.

It has been said that you can tell the consciousness level of people by the books they read. In recent years the best-seller list has included books emphasizing assertiveness, intimidation, selfishness: It's okay to be greedy, and "high-level Machiavellianism" are popular ideas. The books that support these ideas are successful simply because the writers are telling people what they want to hear. People who are lost and confused in a world of extreme material-ism have been asking, "What is life?" and have come up empty. Thus they have concluded, simplistically, that life is getting the most for the least.

Sadly, the field of metaphysical studies has not been ex-empt from this materialistic trend. There has been growing emphasis on this trend by teachers and in scores of books outlining techniques for the demonstration of money and things and position. You can be a millionaire! You can have money, all that you want! Gold-dust blessings! Treat for this, treat for that, treat for anything and everything. Get, get, get is the watchword.

But all this misses a very important point: Life is lived from within-outward, and the purpose of life is not acquisi-tion, but unfoldment and personal development. As long as the emphasis is on getting and not giving there is a sell-ing of one's soul for a "mess of pottage." As the Bible clearly teaches, this leads inevitably to want.

It is possible that one of the causes of this present em-phasis on materialism is attributable to the sad neglect of the teaching of the law of giving in our entire Western culture. Religious institutions have failed people miserably in this respect, partly because they have failed to relate the *act* of giving to the creative flow within the individual, and partly because the churches have been too preoccupied with their own financial support. Little has been taught of the spiritual process of giving. Laying the burden of obligation on people, preachers have talked of giving as a returning of a portion of one's income to God. But this has skirted the issue by dealing with an anemic God in the skies who bargains with us for a giving return.

Jesus said, "Consider the lilies of the field, how they grow" (Mt. 6:28). By nature's law they grow and unfold from bulbs to flowers. But there is no obligation for the flower to return a portion of its life to nature. There is no way it can do so. It can only exude beauty and fragrance and drop seeds into the soil. For life is a forward, growing, unfolding experience. It has been said that our life is God's gift to us; what we do with it is our gift to God (when we freely invest ourselves in creative living and giving).

At this point, we are not thinking of giving as a philanthropic gesture or a monetary contribution to a church. Giving is an aspect of God inherent in all life, like the process of inhaling and exhaling . There is an inexorable cycle of receiving, giving, receiving, giving. The concentric perspective helps us to realize that giving involves inner receiving and that the giving is actually a giving way to the inner flow. The dynamics of giving is so much a part of one's being, of one's I AM-ness, that one must get in sync with the receiving, giving, receiving flow—or stagnate.

In this do-it-yourself age there has been much interest in personal development. This is good. But unfortunately, much of the direction given and the techniques suggested have been exteriorly oriented. With the concept that life is lived from the outside, personal development has implied putting on a winning personality as a mask and conditioning oneself with attitudes that "win friends and influence people."

To *develop* does not mean to add something to your life,

pasting a facade over your limitations. The word *develop* is rooted in concentrics (from within). It is related to *envelop*, meaning "to enclose." *Develop* is just the opposite, generally meaning "to unfold." The bulb develops as it unfolds into the flowering lily. To develop personally should mean to unfold the inner splendor that is God.

So, while the typical self-help course is devoted to the goal of "getting," we are concerned with helping you to understand the science of giving. As we have said, failure to teach this vital science has been a tragic neglect, more serious even than the failure to teach Johnnie to read.

All nature surrounds us with a wonderful world of giving. We have lost our unity with life in the delusive concept that life is to be found and experienced and acquired and amassed from "out there." For most persons most of the time, the focus of consciousness is on getting rather than on giving.

On a commuter train two men were engaged in a spirited conversation. Finally one man blurted out, "Just tell me one thing, what's in it for me?" This may be the hallmark of the level of materialistic consciousness that prevails in today's marketplace.

Having dealt with a cross section of humanity over half a century, I have come to the conclusion that people can be divided into two groups: *takers* and *givers*. Takers believe that life will always be the sum total of what they can *get* from the world. They are forever thinking get, get, get. They plan and scheme ways to get what they want in money, love, happiness, and good of all kinds. But no matter what they get, they never know peace or security or fulfillment.

Givers, on the other hand, are convinced that life is for giving. Their subtle motivations are always concentric, thus focused on giving themselves away in love, service, and all the many ways in which they can invest themselves. They are always secure, for they instinctively know that their good comes, not from the world "where moth and rust consume and where thieves break in and steal" (Mt. 6:19), but from within.

I sincerely hope that somewhere along the way of coming to grips with the ideas of this book, you will see the importance of, and make a deep commitment to, moving out of the *taker* class, preceded by the honest discovery and self-admission that you have been in that class. As you consciously become a giver, I can guarantee that you will experience a miraculous change in your whole life experience, for the law is "give and you will receive."

Life for the whole person is a giving process. I am not just talking about money giving, church giving, tithing, and so on. These are methods and techniques, and we will discuss them later in the book. I am referring to basic principles, fundamental attitudes toward life that may be "outformed" in many different ways. It is the awareness that life is a matter of developing or unfolding from within, that life is not something to *get*, but something to *express*. It is knowing that your real business is the express business, no matter what name your vocation may have.

A picture in my study is titled *The Blessing of Work*, by German artist Rosenthal. It has blessed me with its dynamic message for forty years. The picture depicts a young boy carving a life-size figure of the Virgin Mary. His whole manner suggests a giving of himself to his task in commitment and love. He is using as his model a picture of a woman who, one can assume, is his mother, who looks admiringly upon him. The light streams in the window toward him, and on the wall a plaster plaque depicts an angelic choir singing hosannas to him. While the lad is tenderly working on the feet of the figure, his Virgin Mary looks down upon him in compassion, with outstretched arms over him, blessing him as he works.

What's in it for the boy? This carved figure may bring him fame and fortune, or it could wind up in a dusty attic somewhere. But nothing can ever exceed or detract from the compensation he is receiving in that instant. This is the wonder of giving. It is important to note also that the hand-carved figure could never be duplicated by one who lacks his giving attitude.

"What's in it for me?" you may ask of your work, feeling that you are not adequately compensated. If you can get the perspective of concentrics, you will have a sense of your work as a giving process, and you will be willing to give way to the creative flow, which will lead to better work and, by the law of causation, to greater affluence. But if you still ask the question, "What's in it for me?" then you are being grossly underpaid even if your income is in six figures. If all you get out of your work is a paycheck, you are shortchanging yourself.

One man, whom we will call Dennis Dooley, has very little of what the world calls wealth. But he has far greater wealth, the wealth of Spirit, the spirit of giving of himself as he travels his daily path. He compliments a sad-faced, shabbily dressed woman on the beauty of the crying child in her arms. He greets the office boy with a "thank you, son," when the boy returns with the emptied wastebasket. He gives an encouraging word to the frightened stenographer on her first day at the office. He writes letters to new reporters to congratulate them on a story. He stops off at the drugstore to thank the druggist for his quick delivery of a special order. Once when he learned the paper boy's bicycle had broken down, he offered to drive the boy around his route, even at the end of a hard day at work. Of course everyone loves Dennis Dooley, and all go out of their way to do things for him. He is a giver, not a taker. For, of course, the taker would say, "What's in it for me?"

You may occasionally hear it said (you might even have said it yourself), "My life has no meaning!" This sense of meaninglessness may lead to boredom, depression, fatigue, and even to excessive dependencies and addictions. Actually, it makes about as much sense to say, "My life has no meaning" as it does to stand in a dark cave with an unlit flashlight in your hand and say, "This place has no light!" Jesus would say, "Let *your* light shine!"

Life's meaning is a matter of concentrics. It is not to be found "out there." It is something that you discover and release from within. You put meaning into your work, into your experiences, and into your relationships by the giving attitude in which you meet them. Many people find meaning and interest and excitement in a kind of work that might be a drag to someone else.

If you really apply yourself to the challenges posed by this book, you will catch the idea of concentrics. You will become aware that life flows out from the center within you and that you are "the focus of an Infinite idea." We will deal with the many ways of giving that will provide you with a positive means of changing your life. It is my hope that it will be a retraining process for beginning to think *give* instead of *get*.

Jesus said, "Give, and it will be given to you" (Lk. 6:38). However, this is not a bargaining with a capricious God. It is the articulation of spiritual law. The creative flow in you is a giving process. Your act of giving does not change anything in God, causing Him to sit up and take notice. As you give, you give way to the process, and the result is *as if* God were making a special response just for you.

The divine flow within you requires but one thing of you: your consent to be a receiving channel. It is like a water faucet that must be opened to the flow in order that water may pour forth freely. Jesus is stressing the need to get into a giving consciousness in order to sustain the flow of good in your life. Not just money gifts. He is emphasizing a state of mind. Think *give* and you will *get!* Such thinking will lead to a giving vibration, which is the key to personal prosperity, health, and well-being.

It might be expected that a book dealing with the subject of giving would have some ulterior motives. So please, hear me out. Don't get turned off by a concern that I am making a subtle pitch for your financial support. I am concerned only that you should develop an awareness of, and make a firm commitment to, the cosmic law of causation: "As you give, so do you receive." If you are interested in finding "the better way," become a good giver. Don't delude yourself. Keep your channels open through commitment to some form of systematic giving.

When you discover the wonder of giving, you may well wonder how you could have lived so long in any other way. It is the key that makes Truth work, that opens the door to the good you have been seeking, and that gives life an added glow. It can be one of the great discoveries of your life. When you have become a committed giver, you could no more go back to the old way than you could return to life in prehistoric times.

There is a new world awaiting you, a new level of life open to you, and a new experience of the dynamism of the Truth that you have been experiencing. Get the concentric perspective. Have an occasional meditation when you return in consciousness to the center. Realize that at the center within you the activity of God flows forth *as* you. Concentrically speaking, what you seek is seeking you. Discover the wonder of giving. It is the better way. The day will come when you will insist that it is the only way.

TWO

THAT WHICH COMPELS GOD

We are going to consider a concept that may at first seem paradoxical, even inimical, to the usual metaphysical approach to demonstration, with emphasis on getting money, getting jobs, getting ahead, getting a mate, getting well. Our basic theme is *giving way to life*. But there are many ways to give way. Jesus suggests one in the beatitude, "Blessed are the meek, for they shall inherit the earth" (Mt. 5:5). I like to call this "the science of gentleness."

There is a human tendency that may be found in more of us than might want to admit to it: the willful and persistent effort to get our way. It is, figuratively, to use a battering ram instead of a key to open a door.

Without being aware of what we are doing, we tend to

carry this approach over into our prayer efforts. Jesus says, "When you pray, go into your room and shut the door" (Mt. 6:6). It is an enticing call to inner prayer. But few really find this inner place and the peace and renewal that come through it. We are simply unaware that the door opens outward. Thus we press and push against the door as hard as possible, by affirmations and word treatments, oblivious that we are closing it all the more firmly. The need is to step back and let the divine flow open the door *to* us and *through* us.

Take a moment now to close your eyes and reflect on the concentric perspective. You may want to draw the symbol again in the margin of the page: two cones touching at the points, formed by two straight intersecting lines. Again, in the left cone print in bold letters, "BEING." In the right cone print in smaller letters, "being me." Remember, life may be experienced in many ways and in various states of consciousness, but it can only be *lived* from within-outward. All life, all substance, all love, all wisdom flow forth from within. This is concentrics. Whatever the human need, get still and return in consciousness to that inmost center where the allness of God is becoming the "each-ness" of you.

An Oriental axiom says, "Meekness compels God Himself." It is a great Truth with scientific corroboration. The best conductor of electricity is the substance that is least resistant to the flow of current. One of the greatest breakthroughs of technological history was recently with development of a substance that approaches zero resistance to the conduction of electrical energy. We are told that this amazing substance is going to make revolutionary changes that will affect all our lives. In the same sense, the best conductor of divine power is the person who is nonresistant to the flow. Jesus was referring to a consciousness of zero resistance when He said, in effect, "All things are possible to those who believe."

An experience I had some years ago that has helped me immeasurably in the practice of meditation came while I was exploring the biofeedback process. With electrosensors affixed to my hands, I was told to concentrate on the movement of a needle on a meter. The object was to hold a mental attitude that would cause the needle to go up. I watched carefully as an instructor caused this effect, and I thought to myself, "That should be a breeze; after all, I am a metaphysician!" So I sat quietly for a minute, concentrating all my power, and the needle went down! Like a child threatening to hold his breath, I strained, and the needle continued to go downward. Finally, I regrouped, analyzing the process and how I had been approaching the objective. Suddenly aha! I could see my error. I assumed an extremely relaxed state coupled with an air of complete indifference, but still visualized the needle going up. Lo and behold, the needle did in fact go up. I discovered that I could achieve this result again and again if I would simply let go of the ego desire to demonstrate my great powers, and get myself out of the way. Meekness and gentleness *compelled* the process to work for me.

Again reflect on the concentric perspective. With your thoughts centered at the point of Being being you, there is no limit to the creative flow of life, substance, intelligence, or love. No matter what the condition of life at the circumference of experience, you can find help and healing and overcoming, "not by might, nor by power, but by my Spirit, says the Lord" (Zech. 4:6). The human tendency is to look out there to people, to human resources, to books, to remedies. But the key is to turn within and get centered at the point of oneness. Remember, God can do no more for you than He can do through you. The divine flow requires but one thing of you—your consent to be a believing, nonresistant channel. When you become a positive receptor, the activity of God must flow forth—it can't help itself. For God is life, God is love, God is intelligence, God is substance, not just a capricious presence doling out personal answers. It is such a simple thing, but because of the inertial factor of human consciousness, it is certainly not easy.

One of the exponents of the flow of life was Lao-tzu, who lived centuries before the time of Jesus, which proves that Jesus did not originate the Truth; He simply discovered it and demonstrated it in seemingly miraculous ways.

Here are some thoughts of Lao-tzu (6th century B.C.): "Those who would take over the earth and shape it to their will never, I notice, succeed. The earth is like a vessel so sacred, that at the mere approach, it is marred, and when they reach out their fingers, it is gone. For a time in the world some force themselves ahead, and some are left behind, for a time in the world some make a great noise, and some are held silent, for a time in the world some are puffed fat, and some are kept hungry, for a time in the world some push aboard and some are tipped out . . . . At no time in the world will a man who is sane, overreach himself, overspend himself, overrate himself."

He touches on many relevant themes. For instance, the latter, "overrate himself." The story is told of a time when Gregory Peck, the well-known movie star, was standing in line with a friend, waiting for a table in a crowded restaurant in New York City. The friend, growing impatient with the wait, kept suggesting to Peck, "Why don't you tell the maître d' who you are?" Peck shook his head and wisely observed, "If you have to tell someone who you are, then you aren't."

The chief difference between important people and self-important people is that the former have no need or desire to assert themselves. They rest easily within; and if they strut or push, the effect is to diminish their stature, not to enhance it. What boasters or braggarts cannot seem to recognize is that they are undermining the very image they seek to create in the minds of other people. It is hard to think of any attitude or mask that is as self-defeating as braggadocio, which exposes weakness in the guise of strength. Someone who has authority based on spiritual integrity, who has genuine reserves of power, which come from a concentric perspective, can afford the luxury of good manners, of deferring to others when it is appropriate, of understanding his or her capacities and treating opponents with generosity.

One of the most difficult lessons to learn for ambitious young people is that when you try to make an impression on someone, that is the impression you make. Only those whose emotional focus is deeply centered in the concentric perspective are willing to wait quietly in line until they are recognized.

The word *gentleness* has long gone out of vogue. Wouldn't it be wonderful if it could be rediscovered by modern society? It could neutralize some of the influences of hard rock music and some of the allure of drugs. *Gentleness* means mild, kindly, amiable, not severe or violent. It also has synonyms such as: courteous, tender, compassionate, considerate, tolerant, meek, mild-tempered, tranquil, smooth, calm, and it has a connotation of a person of good birth. These words are rarely found in the lexicon of contemporary usage. What a loss!

At one time *gentleman* and *gentlewoman* had rich meaning, suggesting a person of character, breeding, poise, and dignity—one who has accepted the noblesse oblige that goes with culture.

It is sad that this idea has been eroded by the tendency to "let it all hang out," to "tell it like it is," to be honest (which unfortunately has come to mean to be negative and uncouth) and all this interspersed with a plethora of four-letter words.

The great tragedy is that Homo sapiens is innately a gentle creature and the kind of behavior that is all too common in our day prevents people from really knowing themselves. They simply cover themselves with an appearance of freedom, which cloaks their inner sense of meaninglessness and fear.

Any action or behavior that expresses other than true gentleness is a frustration of potentiality. This frustration is at the root of all personal experiences of sickness, inharmony, or lack. It is the stress and tension that gives rise to what I call "mental cholesterol," that which blocks the flow of the divine creative process within us. This concept has been fundamental to Unity for a hundred years, but it is being given the imprimatur of modern medicine and psychology in these latter days.

One of the saddest things in life is a person's propensity to use force to get his or her way, to use the battering ram instead of the key to open doors. This tendency is at the root of most world conflicts and most personal problems. Heard on the radio this very morning as I wrote this chapter was a news item of yet another case where an irate motorist in California, in an argument over some kind of right-of-way, pulled out a gun and shot and killed another motorist. Commenting on this puzzling phenomenon, a psychologist cited, as we have earlier, the recent interest in books dealing with assertiveness and intimidation as giving rise to much rationalized aggressive behavior. He added that with the unfortunate availability of handguns, many people give vent to spur-of-the-moment acts of hostility, and the concealed gun simply spurs the moment. This same news item reported that more than eighty people were shot in this manner in one year in California alone, twenty of them fatally. A new wave of gentleness and good manners could turn this whole phenomenon around. Certainly it is something that a civilized society cannot tolerate and remain civilized.

Unfortunately, we have thought of gentleness, quietness, humility, and meekness as signs of weakness. Ignorance has obscured the great Truth of our infinite potential.

One of the most misunderstood of Jesus' Beatitudes is, "Blessed are the meek, for they shall inherit the earth." Considered from the perspective of a person living in a hostile world, the statement is ridiculous. It is most certainly the aggressive and not the meek who inherit and possess the earth. In fact, the average individual has many discouraging moments brooding over the great injustices of life, because "they" always seem to get the breaks.

Some have thought that Jesus was talking about a future millennium when these things would come to pass, when the quiet and timid ones will have the upper hand, and the aggressive and overbearing will be rendered impotent. However, let us not forget that Jesus insisted that the kingdom of heaven is at hand! His teachings always dealt with the *now* of experience. You see, we have misunderstood the word *meekness*, and it has been our great loss. For in this beatitude, Jesus gives one of the great keys to power and achievement.

In our self-limiting attitudes of human inferiority we, as individuals, have often thought of ourselves as "me against the world." However, when we learn the art of concentrics, we will discover that life is lived from within-outward, and the great need is to give way to the inner flow and thus to release our greater powers.

Jesus was not talking about meekness as an approach toward people, which could foolishly expose us to aggressive behavior and let people, even *encourage* them, to walk all over us. No, His meekness was concentric, dealing with the within—an attitude toward God. Jesus was meek toward God. He knew that "I of myself can do nothing." He was just a simple carpenter's son who had found His spiritual unity with God. In this discovery He had tapped the secret of the universe. But He knew that the great power that accrued to Him was concentric in that it came not to Him but through Him from the inner center. His well-deserved title of "Master" came to Him because He knew that as long as He kept centered, He could do all things, and all because He *did* keep centered.

In my early years, I seriously studied voice at a music conservatory. I aspired to a career as a vocalist. One of my ideals was the great tenor Roland Hayes. I saw him in concert on many occasions. I was always impressed by his custom of coming to the stage and, as the applause faded, facing the audience, with his eyes closed and in complete silence for what seemed like minutes but was probably only a few seconds. He was once asked by a reporter in an interview what this silent period was about, what was he thinking or doing? A humble man, Hayes was hesitant to reveal his secret. But after persistent probing, he admitted that he was praying. On being pressed further, he said, "I simply get quiet and pray, 'Oh Lord, blot out Roland Hayes, that the people may hear only Thee.' " Indeed, to me, it was as if the very voice of God was singing through him. The humble prayer of Roland Hayes was the meekness that compelled God.

If you have a presentation to make or an important conversation with your superior, let go of the ego (which is very much involved if you are experiencing fear). Assume the concentric perspective, the attitude of giving way to the flow of power, which Jesus said it is the Father's good pleasure to give you.

The Greek word *praeis*, which we have translated as meek, has the connotation of "tamed," from the standpoint of harnessing that which is wild and unrestrained. Niagara Falls is an example of raw and unrestrained power. Tremendous forces are involved as the Niagara River dashes madly over the falls. This vast energy was wasted for millions of years until we built several large power plants to harness the power to generate electricity. Today the falls have been tamed as the water turns giant turbines to generate electrical energy for many cities. The meekness of Niagara Falls has inherited earth. This suggests a manner of reserve and control, of poise and peacefulness. However, it is not weakness, but strength, for all the inner powers are harnessed in reserve, not dissipated in bluster and show.

It is interesting that the French translation of the Bible renders this beatitude, "Blessed are the debonair." This gives a whole new dimension of meaning. *Debonair* means "of pleasant manner, courteous, gracious, charming, and carefree." This might suggest the contemporary word *cool*. Blessed are the cool—those who have it all together. When you are cool, you don't have to get your way by using bluster and show. Your coolness projects a positive power that goes much farther than any amount of force, assertiveness, or aggressiveness.

The meek person, in the context that Jesus used the word, has a lot of *give* inside. This individual has the capacity to give way. Arguments don't have to be won for "the principle of the thing." For he or she knows that the true principle of the thing is a supportive process. Thus, the meek individual can easily give in, give way, even give up—for the sake of harmony.

A person may say, "But I am fighting for my good name." But if you really have a good name, it needs no defense. To fight for it is to reveal your insecurity and self-doubts. If you are centered in the concentric perspective and someone makes a slur against you or impugns your character, instead of lashing out in defense, you can quietly say to yourself, "It is interesting that this person feels that way. I wonder what is disturbing him or her?" In other words, it is not a question of what is said about you, but rather why you are disturbed by what is said.

You see, Jesus, in saying "blessed are the meek," is implying, blessed are those who keep centered within. When you are centered, you know when to step back, to give way, when to go on might simply be willful. Those who are centered don't borrow trouble by insisting on rights or fighting for freedom. They know that the only truly free people are those who keep their hearts free from hatred and conflict.

Dynamic people have been characterized as aggressive, domineering, and flamboyant, those who thunder through life. But truly dynamic people are not noisy. They are meek in the sense of having it all together, their powers in control, their consciousness centered. They can speak with authority and take decisive action with power and conviction. But they don't beat the drum. Instead of thundering, they use the lightning of ideas. Instead of cursing the darkness, they turn on the light.

Whatever obstacle you may face in life, the need is to turn within and get centered in the divine flow. Instead of pressing and straining for an answer, relax in an attitude of gentleness and love. Now please note, I am not talking about weakness or passivity or indolence or procrastination. I am talking about life that is together, talents that are harnessed, powers that are focused, and a manner that is cool.

In our quest for world peace, perhaps it is time to be nationally debonair, cool, controlled. It may be important to carry the "big stick," as Teddy Roosevelt urged, but he also emphasized the need to speak softly. For then we will not stew over who has the most bombs. We will seek to be the most human, the most loving, the most gentle.

E. Stanley Jones tells of seeing a little, frail flower growing in the vast ruins of ancient Babylon. He wondered, how could this little flower, so frail that he could crush it in his fingers, have survived, while this vast empire founded on military might perished? He realized it was because the flower obeyed the laws of God written within itself. It lived. The empire disobeyed those laws. It perished. The flower follows the way of nature's gentleness. The nation perished by its own militaristic doctrine.

In the attempt to deal with all the confusions and conflicts in the world today, gentleness is a creative alternative. It is in the concentric perspective that, in our Sunday meetings of creative "worth-ship" in New York's Avery Fisher Hall, a great assembly nearly three thousand strong, we close the meeting by singing: "Let there be peace on earth, and let it begin with me."

Let there be justice in the company I work for, and let it begin with my work ethic. Let there be honesty and integrity in the functions of government, and let it begin with my willingness to obey its laws. Let there be love and harmony within all people and all nations, and let it begin in the loving and harmonious way I live. For it is the attitude that compels God.

THREE

KEY TO A STRESS-FREE LIFE

One of the most widespread problems of modern times is what is often called the "pressure syndrome." Certainly most of us are all too familiar with the high-level tension seemingly built into life and work, causing stress and all sorts of compound problems of mind and body.

There are many situations in which we may typically respond with stress: a multimillion dollar financial crunch for a business executive; an accumulation of bills to pay with the oftentimes inadequate take-home pay of the average worker; two term papers due on the same day for the student; a make-or-break audition for a musician or actor. When pressures exceed our limits, creativity disappears, errors multiply, and new challenges have to be met with tired replays of old strategies. Life becomes jittery and unpleasant, and subject to a wide range of physical ills.

This word *stress* is heard so often today that it would almost appear to be some new disease. As a matter of fact, the early caveman trying to live in a world dominated by giant creatures and unpredictable elements probably experienced great stress. No, stress is nothing new.

But the thing that is becoming more and more widely accepted is that the "stress response" actually frustrates the flow of life and thus is at least a partial cause of most physical ills, perhaps all of them. Of course it has been difficult for the medical profession to let go of the deep-seated physical orientation, the insistence that physical ailments are produced by physical causes and should be treated by physical intervention.

However, continued research into E.I.I. (emotionally induced illness) and stress has shown undeniable mind-body relations. But there is an ego "thing" in the medical community that is understandable, and so the medical field has accepted E.I.I. under a medical orientation, with a "new" science and a new twenty-one letter, nine syllable word: *psychoneuroimmunology*. Today, whether the physician or the metaphysician is talking, the advice may be the same: "Let go of stress!" But the question is, how?

There are many "surefire" methods offered by popular writers on the subject: from hypnotic suggestion, to chucking it all to go and paint or write in far-off Tahiti, with possible misadventures with Valium along the way. Actually the answer is as close as the creative use of the imagination. For stress is not produced by things that occur. It is the thought and feeling about them that gives that gnawing, head-in-the-vise feeling.

There is an old adage, "When things get tight, something's got to give!" For many people this has meant that the chain is no stronger than its weakest link, and that in the midst of conflict we may have a breakdown, or hit the ceiling, or lose our job, or experience some tragic loss.

However, with the perspective of concentrics, we can see that it means, "Give way to life." In other words the tightness is the result of pressures within us that may have been building up because of the way we have been dealing with things. "Something has to give" may not mean some dire explosion or catastrophe, but may imply something *to do*. Know that your good flows from within, so give way.

Jesus said, "I have said this to you, that in me you may have peace. In the world you have tribulation; but be of good cheer, I have overcome the world" (Jn. 16:33). This word *tribulation* comes from the Latin *tribulum* which means "press." In other words, in the world you have pressures, but I have found the way to overcome them.

One of the most important things Jesus taught was that the only problems you ever have are in your own mind: "A man's foes will be those of his own household" (Mt. 10:36). No matter what happens out there in the world, or even on your doorstep, all that really counts is what happens in your own mind. When you get your thoughts centered at the still point within and begin to see your life as a giving experience, then you control the giving, and no one can take that control from you.

If you become irritable, tense, and easily overwhelmed, what you need is not a coffee break, but a prayer break, a time for silence. Right where you are—at your desk, at the kitchen sink, even driving your car—take a few deep breaths to establish the image of life glowing from within. Whisper to yourself: *I am free from tension, stress, and strain.* Then with your vision sharpened with the concentric

27

perspective, go on your way doing what you are doing. This simple process of getting centered within is the finest strategy for coping.

There is one fundamental that I feel we should call to mind often: You always have a choice! In everything that happens to you, you have a choice. You don't have to get angry. You don't have to be fearful. You don't have to become jealous. You have a choice, whether to curse the darkness or bring a light, whether to engage in fretting or letting, whether to experience tension and stress in the face of things or keep centered in the poise and strength of the Christ mind within.

One man made this great discovery of poise and power at the center. He reminds himself in the face of problems that arise in his life: "I am bigger than anything that can happen to me. All these things — sorrow, misfortune, suffering — are outside my door. I am in the house, and I have the key." And that key is giving way to life! In other words, "I am in charge."

When you are centered in the concentric perspective, aware that life is lived from within-outward, and that *you* control the giving, you can walk easily through any and all experience out there without conflict or pressure. But if you lose your inner center and become immersed in things in your work, you will be pushed and pulled, and you will feel lost, for you will have no roots.

There is a self-treatment that I have found to be effective in coping with a stressful response to conditions: *I work without strain and walk without hurry, for I am in tune with the rhythm of the universe. That which needs to be accomplished will be done at the right and perfect time and in the right and perfect way.*

Without inner centering, you may forever seek proof

that your life is secure. There is pressure in trying to get what you want, the fear of losing what you have, and the general concern that your very existence is threatened. All this because you believe that your life is something you have acquired, rather than something you are experiencing as a result of what you have given way to.

One man was under constant pressure to get ahead, to be a success, and to have all the things that spelled affluence: a lovely home, expensive cars, and all the luxuries money could buy. He achieved all these ends. From a material standpoint, he was at the pinnacle of success. But strangely, he was always beset with pressures. He had certainly "made it," but he was beset with a strange sense of not being worthy of it. Thus, he was plagued with the relentless urge to work harder to prove to himself that he was, after all, a success. But the pressures continued, giving rise to ulcers and heart and circulatory problems. He was on constant medication and under doctor's care.

One day at his office an emergency call brought the alarming report that his home was on fire. He dashed out of the office and drove furiously to his surburban residence; but, alas, by the time he arrived, there was nothing left but charred ruins. It was a traumatic and painful experience, and he had a very stressful night.

But the next morning the sun rose to herald a new day, and the man somehow was possessed of a new perspective. Raking through the ashes, he realized how he had totally lost his sense of values. He said to himself, "Everything has gone up in smoke, but so what? All these evidences of affluence have come to me because of what has come *through* me. Life is still very much a matter of giving way to the inner flow. Actually everything that is really important to me remains. I have my wife and my children. I have my mind. I still have the ability by which all this was achieved. I still have the future. So I will go forth in a giving consciousness, and I know that my way will be bright and wonderful." Suddenly he was free from the load that he had been carrying for years. He made a new beginning, but this time consciously working from his inward center, in the realization of giving, rather than frantic getting. In the ensuing years he has recouped all the seeming losses, but he is a different person—calm, poised, imperturbable, and truly free.

Often the cause of pressure and stress is the burden of responsibilities associated with our work. One man, in a letter requesting prayer help, explained how something was threatening to cut short his career. By hard work and commitment to his employer, he had made a meteoric rise to a high executive position in an important corporation. However, he carried a heavy burden of having to make frequent snap decisions involving countless millions of dollars. Just one bad decision could cost the company a fortune. He would often lie awake at night, second-guessing the judgments made that day. He said that he very nearly broke under the strain. Then someone gave him a copy of one of my books, and he was introduced to what I am calling the concentric process, the concept that life is lived from within-outward. He caught the idea of guidance as spiritual law, not divine caprice. He discovered the great truth that he didn't have to make decisions, he only had to give way to the intuitive flow and let the decisions happen. He wrote to tell of his gratitude for this simple concept that had turned his life around.

What this man proved was that conditions do not cause the stress, but our response to them, how we deal with them causes stress. Now this man casts his burden on the

Lord. This means that he works confidently in the awareness that the Father knows what things he needs even before he asks Him. The right solution, the perfect choice, leading to the best possible decision, is known in you, and will flow forth through you if you will only give way to it. The man now knows that he needs never to make a decision. The key is to discover the decision, and let the decision make him.

Some interesting research on this subject was done at the Du Pont company, probing whether it is true that executives are at high risk for heart attacks because of the great pressures under which they work. The study revealed that executives and plant managers had an annual heart attack rate of only 2.2 per 1,000, while the manual worker rate is 3.2 per 1,000, and the clerical worker rate is 4.0 per 1,000. It just could be that people become executives precisely because of their ability to withstand stress.

In other words, the tensions of responsibility do not necessarily shorten an individual's life. As the research report summed it up, "Stress cannot be measured by the external circumstances with which a person must contend, but rather by his reaction to these circumstances. One person's stress may be another person's pleasure."

I once stood before the beautiful statue of Jesus created by the Danish sculptor Thorvaldsen. There is an interesting story told about how the statue came into being in its present form. It seems that the artist wanted to make the greatest figure ever made of Jesus. He formed a commanding figure of great strength, with a fine, well-shaped head thrown back imperiously, with arms raised in a gesture of domination and command. When the artist departed for home for the night, he left the window open to facilitate the hardening of the clay. However, during the night the fog and wet sea mist caused the clay to sag and the arms and head to slump. When Thorvaldsen returned the next morning, he found the head had fallen slightly, and now looked down with an expression of compassion, and the arms were no longer raised in a gesture of command but were lowered in an attitude that suggested giving. The figure still showed great power, but instead of a pose of domination over things of the world, it now expressed a sense of the flow of love and service, a feeling of giving way. The artist at first was greatly disappointed. But as he sat reflecting on the change, it slowly dawned upon him that this was what he had really meant to portray. So he titled the figure *Come Unto Me*.

In a very real sense, this is what happens when we become centered in the Christ consciousness. It softens the features made hard by materialistic thinking and relaxes the muscles made taut by the stress response, by the emphasis on get, get, get.

The physical pose of people engaged in making a living and carving out a place in the world may well be symbolized by the first conception that the artist had of Jesus — commanding, assertive, and willful. Life for such people is all push and pull and struggle and strain. They have an attitude that often displays brash confidence. They may even achieve a kind of success. But it is built on the sands of materiality. As Jesus points out, the house built on sand will fall under the pressure of crises.

But when Truth comes into your consciousness, when you get the concentric perspective of life that is lived from within-outward, there is an almost spontaneous relaxing of your human hold on life and things and relationships. Work becomes a giving process. You are in tune with the free flow of substance.

Again, "when things get tight, something's got to give." A powerful kind of giving is giving thanks. You may think of thankfulness as a feeling that comes after changes for the better, rather than before them. You might consider it to be impossible, or at least Pollyannaish, to stop and feel grateful in a tense and critical situation. Gratitude comes from the Latin *gratus*, which means pleasing, and *itude*, which means a quality or state of mind. So literally *gratitude* means an attitude of pleasure. You will recall that Jesus said, "It is your Father's good pleasure to give you the kingdom" (Lk. 12:32).

Turn again to the symbol of concentrics, with the two cones touching at the points, formed by two intersecting lines. Recall that the cone on the left suggests the whole universe in focus as you, and the cone on the right suggests the cosmic center in you opening out into the expression that you are physically, mentally, and emotionally. At that point of oneness there is a relentless creative flow of life, substance, intelligence, and boundless creativity. I like to hold the image of the whole of Divine Mind, infinite love, and limitless substance relentlessly seeking to flow forth to meet any and all needs, and even before we ask. The divine "givingness" is always ready, and the attitude of gratitude is the most powerful key by which to get into the giving consciousness. Thus, when things get tight and something's got to give, start giving thanks, stir up the attitude of gratitude.

It is interesting that much stress comes from the subtle loss of priorities in the things for which we are working. Thus, we act for all the world as if life begins and ends in excelling at this job, getting that promotion, catching a particular train, winning this bridge game, or meeting the business deadline. This tends to keep us under constant pressure, fighting time, resisting change, and dealing with people who may be working under a different set of priorities.

This is one of the drawbacks of having clearly set goals and well-outlined master plans. For unless you are careful, they can produce great pressures. Certainly have a plan, and keep it in the back of your mind. But don't worry about it. This moment is all you have. The past is behind you. The future is still to come. A goal is not a preoccupation for tomorrow but a direction for today.

One of the common causes of pressure for the student of Truth is the problem of perfectionism. Truth is an ultimate. Perfection is a direction for today's unfoldment, not a static condition to achieve. Robert Browning says, "A man's reach should exceed his grasp, or what's a heaven for?" Certainly keep on, and keep on keeping on. But be patient with yourself and with others. Give yourself and others frequent pats on the back. Remember how far you have come, not how far you are from the summit of perfection. Certainly reach high and expect much from life and from yourself. But you have all eternity to achieve your goal. As Josiah G. Holland says, "Heaven is not reached in a single bound, but we build the ladder by which we rise from lowly earth to vaulted skies, and we mount to its summit round by round."

Perfectionists are unreasonably hard on themselves. Something has to give. Be satisfied enough to be happy, but discontent enough to keep working on yourself. A large part of the spiritual quest is the experience of joy, which we can never know if we make our efforts toward achievement grim and tense.

Something has to give! Take an occasional time of centering to get a new sense of what you are about. When

Jesus said, "You, therefore, must be perfect, as your heavenly Father is perfect" (Mt. 5:48), He was not setting an impossible goal that we must struggle hopelessly toward. The Greek word translated as *perfect* is *teleios*, meaning fulfilled, completed. So "be perfect" can be interpreted to mean fulfill yourself; complete the work you are called to do. It does not mean to complete your eternal work of achieving the full stature of the Christ self of you. It means to get it together and fulfill your present uniqueness.

When the rich young ruler asked Jesus what thing he should do to have eternal life, Jesus answered, "If you would be perfect, go, sell what you possess and give to the poor" (Mt. 19:21). The things He suggested were immediate and quite possible to do. They were difficult for the young man because "he had great possessions," or, more likely, possessions had him. Life for him was a getting process, and he was unable to transcend his dependency on the fruits of his getting. Jesus was simply saying, "Life is for giving. Prove your willingness to give, and you will fulfill your uniqueness. Something has to give." But the young man was unable.

It is important to establish a habit of taking time at the beginning of every day to get centered within at the still point. Reflect on the realization that life is a giving process, from within-outward. What will be the result of such a daily discipline? You will walk easily through any and all experiences without stress.

Watch your pressure points, and when things get tight and something's got to give, give way and let the creative flow unfold in your life in healthful, prosperous, and fulfilling ways.

FOUR

GIVING
AND FORGIVING

The goal that we have set for ourselves in this book is to turn our lives around by turning around the attitude that life is a getting process. Society has conditioned us to this approach to life and living, and it will require disciplined effort to break the pattern and build on the realization that life is lived from within-outward.

An extremely helpful way to get into a giving consciousness is to release yourself from the bondage of unforgiveness. Just imagine what life would be like if you were to accumulate all the grievances, hurt feelings, and all the injustices that come along in the course of one year! Your load would be impossibly heavy. Actually, there are people who labor under such loads, with disastrous psychological and physical effects. Since most if not all of the physical ills experienced in the body are psychosomatically induced, and more and more medical researchers are coming to this conclusion, the matter of unforgiveness may involve the major culprit of human ills of mind and body. Significantly one researcher calls arthritis "bottled hurt."

Now, of course, most of us don't carry this whole load of the year's unforgiveness, simply because there is a tendency to practice what I call "safety-valve forgiveness." We say, "Oh, well, what's the use?" So we let go out of a sense of the futility of it all. The sensible person comes, in time, to the awareness that willfully insisting upon endlessly carrying hurt or a sense of being wronged inflicts needless damage. So we say, "I give up!"

But, how much better to bless things and people as the situations occur, rather than wait to act as a last resort. This is why Jesus advised us to quickly agree with our adversary. This is often misunderstood as a sign of weakness. But you see, to agree as Jesus used the term does not mean to give in even if it goes against your best interest or highest ideals. In Jesus' usage the word *adversary* refers not to a person but to your adverse thought about a person. Thus, to "agree with" means to "settle with," to deal creatively with the situation—to bless it and let it go.

This dynamic insight is practical Christianity at its very best. It is sad that as churches emphasize what is called "the social gospel" such personal insights are overlooked. Paul said, "Do not let the sun go down on your anger" (Eph. 4:26). At the close of the day, perhaps as you lie in bed before dropping off to sleep, consciously take stock of the mental baggage that you are carrying. Bless each experience; forgive the individuals involved; loose it all and let it go. This may seem difficult, even impossible, where there have been deep grievances. "So-and-so doesn't deserve my love," you may say. But the most important thing is that you deserve it.

One of the most important statements made by Emmet Fox, who made some great ones, is this: "When you hold resentment against anyone, you are bound to that person by a cosmic link, a real tough mental chain. You are tied by a cosmic tie to the thing that you hate. The one person, perhaps in the whole world, whom you most dislike, is the very one to whom you are attaching yourself, by a hook that is stronger than steel."

What a fantastic insight! We use the expressions "hooked on sports" or "hooked on drugs" to imply an addiction. But have you ever thought that you might be hooked on bitterness, resentment, or unforgiveness? You may be unaware of this unconscious hooking of some person or experience within yourself. You may have a long-standing grievance with someone or some organization. You may feel very badly about the grievance, and you may long for relief. Forgiveness is the only way to be free. There is only one way to forgive—by love. It may be a difficult lesson. Let's think about it.

In human relations trenchant remarks and insinuations are often dropped freely. Most of us know what it is to feel such barbs. The thoughtful student of Truth will ask the question, "What can I do to avoid being upset by such things?" Not, "Why do they say or do things like that?" but "Why do I get disturbed by them?"

Do you recall the first time you tried to catch a baseball? You held your arms rigid, and when the ball reached your hands, you grabbed at it tightly as though fighting it. This resulted in bruised fingers or stinging hands, and usually a dropped ball. But when you eventually learned the correct technique, you held your arms loose, and when the ball touched your hands, you grasped it gently but firmly and allowed your arms to give slightly with the forward motion of the ball.

Don't pass over this illustration too hastily. Get the image strongly in mind of painlessly catching the hard ball by *giving way* slightly. Just as you can catch that ball without hurting your hands, you can receive harsh words, whatever they are and whomever they are from, without hurt feelings. It is simply a matter of learning to give with the forward motion of these verbal missiles. If you resist them, they are bound to hurt. But if you keep your emotions flexible, you absorb the sting without injuring yourself.

One of the most difficult jobs is working as custodian of a church, because custodians work for hundreds of "bosses," all telling the custodians what they should be doing. One man distinguished himself in such a job. He was nonresistant and cool. I asked him one day how he was able to do his work so easily without being distracted by all his bosses. He said, "Oh, it's really easy. When people try to push me around, I just put it in neutral and let them push!" As a Quaker gentleman said about working with or around disturbing people, "Why should I let them decide how I am going to think or feel or act?" Why indeed!

It is interesting that the term that best describes this process of giving with the forward motion of a verbal thrust is found in the two words *giving* and *forward*. In her book, *Lessons in Truth*, H. Emilie Cady says, "To forgive is to give for." It is to give some actual good in return for evil received. When we take offense, we are held out of the flow of life. When we forgive, we *for*-give, we get into the upward, progressive, forward movement of life.

Sometimes the hook of unforgiveness becomes a family feud that may go on for years. The classic example is the feud between the Hatfields and McCoys. A squabble began with some offense taken between families. It continued for years until it became a war in which they shot and killed one another, making life miserable for both clans. It is unlikely that in later generations they had the slightest idea of what prompted the dispute, but they all faithfully perpetuated it.

I have known parents and children or siblings to be estranged for years over some upset that led to a hurt and deteriorated into a matter of pride. They never spoke to one another for years. It is a tragic waste!

Two women, next-door neighbors, had a dispute over something quite trivial. For ten long years these women, who had been good friends and in their lonely lives desperately needed this friendly link, didn't speak or acknowledge one another's presence.

In the local paper there was a very popular and widely read column of opinion exchange. One day there appeared a letter expressing some views on a particular subject. It was signed "Arbutis." In a few days there was a letter expressing another opinion on the same issue, signed, "Seagull." Thus began a frequent exchange of comments by Arbutis and Seagull. It went on for ten years. In a pen-pal sort of way this woman, Arbutis, developed a warm friendship with the other person, Seagull. They had a delightful sharing of thoughts for years.

Now when one of the neighbors suddenly died, the other woman felt it was charitable and neighborly to offer to help. While helping a niece straighten up some personal effects, she ran across all the clippings from the paper with the Arbutis and Seagull material. Suddenly the woman who had called herself Arbutis realized that her long-estranged neighbor was actually Seagull. Her "best friend" during all these years had been the one whom she had thought was her worst enemy.

We have discussed the idea that when things get tight, something's got to give. Often the thing that stands in our way is some bit of unforgiveness that we may be hooked on. Jesus always seems to go right to the heart of the matter. He says that if you come to the altar to pray and you remember that you have something against your brother, you should first go and make up with your brother and then come with your gift. In other words, if you are blocking the flow by your resentment or bitterness, not even God can break through with the good you desire. In "The Lord's Prayer" Jesus says, "Forgive us our debts, as we also have forgiven our debtors" (Mt. 6:12). This does not imply bargaining with God. God makes no deals. It means that we must give way to receive. We must let go of indignation and offense if we want to loosen the restrictions in our lives. Something's got to give. There is a great probability that in the case of physical or mental or financial problems in your life, there is some kind of rancor or bitterness or memory of wrong in your consciousness. Something's got to give.

Of course, resentment and hostility often run deep, and forgiveness is not always easy. One may hear many people echoing Peter's objections to Jesus' idealistic teaching: How many times should I forgive a person who does evil to me; seven times? Jesus responded: I am not telling you seven times, but seventy times seven. Peter is saying, "You just can't go on forgiving people. How much can one be expected to take?" Jesus is pointing out that we are dealing with law and not caprice. If you want light in the room, you must turn on the switch and keep it on — or you will have to sit in darkness.

You may feel that forgiving someone who has despitefully used you is just too much to expect, that you have good reason for turning off the light, and a perfect right to your indignation. That is all very well in the logic of human consciousness, but it overlooks the principle. You are a spiritual being, created in and of love, with the "same mind that was in Christ Jesus." But the power and privilege that go with your divinity are yours only when you act the part. Jesus said, "Love your enemies and pray for those who persecute you, so that you may be sons of your Father" (Mt. 5:44-45). Love, so that you may actually be what you innately are. Unforgiveness of any kind frustrates your divine potential. The difference between Jesus and you and me is not that He was created under some special dispensation, but that He acted constantly at the level of His divinity, while we act and react much of the time at the level of our humanity.

But we can change. We can grow. We can be what we are created to be.

Jesus said, "Judge not, that you be not judged" (Mt. 7:1). This is not easy, for how can we see a thing at all without some kind of judgment? In time we may discover that we can. It calls for seeing people not through our prejudices, which Paul calls "seeing in a mirror darkly," but through what Jesus calls "right judgment." It is dealing with all people, experiences, and things from a concentric perspective. It is the "namaskar" consciousness — seeing from the within of you to the within of the others. The question, "How can I forgive after what this individual has done to me?" is answered, "You really don't need to. Get yourself out of the way, and let God forgive through you."

If you judge the wrongs of others, *you* will have to forgive them, for your judgment binds you to a restrictive flow of life, love, and intelligence. Thus, forgiveness of others depends on self-forgiveness. For when you see limitation, you see from a limited perspective, which is a sense of limitation in yourself.

Imelda Shanklin, one of Unity's great teachers, gives an important prayer test. She says, in effect, "Father forgive *me* for expecting in the human that which is found only in the divine." Note, "forgive *me*." In other words, I have sinned by expecting in the human of the person something that can be found only in the Christ within the individual. I must take responsibility for my attitudes.

If we relate to others on a purely human level, there is bound to be an unconscious expectation of human limitations. Our view will be prejudiced. We sometimes say, "That's about what I expected from that character!" The sin is really in the eye of the beholder. The forgiveness must come through understanding—not setting it right, but seeing it rightly.

This may imply a Pollyanna attempt to sweep things under the rug. Not at all! Actually, it is looking carefully at all evils, but staying mindful that we live in a world of our own thinking. Unless we change our thinking or curb the beast within us, we can never do much about the beast out there.

You may say it is impossible to forgive some things. I agree that in human consciousness many things are impossible to forgive. Jesus suggests the step that opens the way. Using one of His classic metaphors, He advises, turn the other cheek. Turn to the other side of your nature, from the human to the divine. Forgiveness is impossible in human consciousness, but very possible and manageable in spiritual consciousness. When you return to the center of your being, you not only let go of unforgiveness, but of the need to forgive. You let go and let the forgiving love of God forgive through you.

Now let us not oversimplify. This practice of forgiveness does not come easily, especially if we or our loved ones have been hurt by the actions of others. It is difficult enough in the minor things of life. When it comes to the big things, such as tragedies, the way of forgiveness is a hard road, but an absolutely necessary one. Remember that we are talking about concentric forgiveness, that which flows through you, not just from you. Like bringing light into a dark room, you do not have to create the light, but you have to flip the switch or open the curtains.

You may say, "They do not deserve my love!" But what about you? Don't you deserve the unbroken circuit of love keeping your life in the flow of good? You may even cry out, "This is too serious a matter to forgive!" Then it is too serious a matter not to forgive.

Let me tell you about a couple whose child was struck down on the street by a hit-and-run driver. These parents had been devoted to this, their only child. With her death, something went out of them. They virtually stopped living. The man became economically impotent. He went through the motions in his business, but everything went against him until it collapsed into bankruptcy. Both of them had great physical suffering, reducing them to pitiful creatures living in a self-imposed prison of hatred, resentment, grief, and fear. They became recluses.

The great need was to give way to life, not to the life that came through their child, but to the life that always flows forth from within. These unfortunate people had lived their lives through their child, thus cutting themselves off, in consciousness, from the divine flow. A child could be, and in their case had been, taken. But nothing could really take them out of the flow of universal life but their own blocked consciousness. Obviously, meeting such a tragedy calls for some spiritual growth. But even before the new perception on which to go through, even grow through, the personal tragedy, it is important to see how illogical it is to meet the destruction of one life with the destruction of two additional ones. Somehow that doesn't seem to be in keeping with the economy of the universe.

This does not mean that one should forgive a wrong while it is being committed; that would be condoning and supporting the wrong. Of course, condemn the act; but forgive the actor. Don't misunderstand, the forgiveness is not for the individual committing the act—it is for you. There is a universal law in which the lawbreaker must ultimately pay the price. "Vengeance is mine . . . says the Lord [law]" (Rom. 12:19). You cannot keep yourself in the flow of good if you hold another in unforgiveness. Don't get caught up in the hook.

Continued unforgiveness for some extreme act is often rationalized as "righteous indignation." The act may have long been stopped, and the darkness of consciousness of the evil one long since corrected. But righteous or unrighteous, if you keep holding to the memory of the wrong, it is you who are now breaking the law.

Two Hindu priests were on a long walking trip. They encountered a river, and as they made ready to cross they came upon a woman in distress, for she feared making the crossing. Despite their priestly vows never to touch a woman, one of the priests took pity on the woman and carried her across on his shoulders. For miles after they resumed their journey, the second priest berated the first one for breaking his vow. Finally, fed up with the constant nagging, the first priest said, "My brother, I simply carried the damsel across the stream and promptly put her down. You have been carrying her for the past twenty miles."

This has shocking implications for those who may be carrying the burden of unforgiveness over wrongs committed or injustices done to them. Certainly we all have to deal with our thoughts about what we see out there in the world, such as acts of terrorism by individuals and groups, and wholesale aggression by warring nations. It is easy to justify feelings of righteous indignation. But again, "Vengeance is mine . . . says the Lord." Under the law of consciousness, a person or group may seem to get away *with* something, but no one can get away *from* the law. In consciousness there is always a price to pay, though you may not see how or when. When disciples would ask Jesus about those people or that situation, He would say, "What is that to you; you follow me." In one of the "Seven Last Words of Jesus" from the Cross, Jesus said, "Father, forgive them; for they know not what they do" (Lk. 23:34). How could He have forgiven such an unjust thing? But that's just it, He didn't forgive! There was no unforgiveness in Him. If Jesus had been smoldering with bitterness and resentment, He would have been earthbound, bound to the perpetrators by a cosmic link, attached by a hook stronger than steel. Thus there could have been no resurrection. Only a soul entirely free and unhampered could have accomplished the final overcoming as Jesus accomplished it.

I am certainly not saying that forgiveness is achieved easily by an act of will. You do not forgive just by saying, "All right, I am going to forgive this thing." You will probably be saying it through your teeth and with fists clenched, implying, "I'll do it if it kills me!"

The only kind of forgiveness that has meaning is concentric. It is not something you have to do, but something you must allow to flow through you. It is to pass from judgment to understanding. It is remembering that life is lived from within-outward, and that personal growth is in the laboratory of human experience. Thus what happens to you must be a reflection of where you happen to be in consciousness. If you don't like what has happened, you need to alter where you are in thought. If you hit back or mentally resist and resent, you close off your inner growth. You extinguish the light, which is your only means of recovery.

The desire for retaliation is one of the most dangerous lusts that enslaves human beings. When you want to hurt one who hurts you, you are asking for something that irritates you while you want it, disappoints you when you get it, and makes you feel mean when it's all over.

When you stop dealing with things at the circumference of experience and from the consciousness of the human, and you let the divine express through the love that has always been the reality of you, giving way to the divine flow, suddenly you have the whole universe on your side.

Practice forgiveness often! I have heard this question by students of Truth: "Should a person pray when he has nothing to pray about?" This implies a misunderstanding of the science of prayer, a failure to realize that life is an experience of growth. You can always have a quiet session in forgiveness. Turn within and get centered in oneness with the creative flow. Visualize the logo of concentrics, the two cones touching at the points. In the one cone see the words *Divine Love*, and in the other one see the words *being your love*. When you are centered and still, feel the radiant and warm rays of that cosmic flow of love dissolving all hurt, all bitterness, all sense of injustice. See this love flow being projected into your world, loving and forgiving all people with whom you have any enmity. Thus with concentric love and forgiveness, you dissolve all the hooks that may have held you in bondage. Remember, forgiveness is not something you have to do, you only have to let it be done.

When humankind as a whole decides that it is fed up with walls of separation and the wars that result, the walls will come down. Men and women will begin to emphasize likenesses instead of differences. People will build bridges instead of complaining about the gaps in understanding and credibility, and turn on lights instead of cursing the darkness. But don't wait for the millennium. Learn the art of giving and forgiving now.

FIVE

CONCENTRICS AND LOVE

Life begins for all of us in the shock of emerging from the security of the womb into a world of insecurity. We are suddenly desperately dependent on others and on the co-operation of the outside world, which does not always cooperate. We find ourselves in a strange dilemma. We are innately gregarious creatures, and yet we have feelings of paranoia. We become increasingly interdependent on people, and yet we feel that we are in competition with them. There is a growing sense that our prosperity, our happiness, even our health depend on what happens in the world around us. Life becomes a matter of watching to see that no one threatens our position or tampers with our rights, and of doing battle with those who do.

When we live from outside-in, life tends to become a matter of things that happen to us, events that occur, things that people say and do. We find that the tone of our lives is completely set from the outside. More than this, we become "other-directed," and we are always on the defensive. Anyone has the power to push our buttons of anger, fear, and hostility.

This leads to the problems of loneliness and friendlessness. Very lonely people will invariably think that they would not be lonely if people would just be friendlier, kinder, and more loving to them. But the fact is that they are lonely because they have lost their center. Lonely people will always be lonely. You may give them a party to cheer them up and to introduce them to new friends. But in the end, "poor, lonely Fred" may be found sitting in the corner talking to no one because he is lonely. He is lonely because he is frustrating his own divine flow.

As a spiritual being you always have the freedom to love. For one who is living a life seemingly devoid of love, to talk about the "freedom to love" is about like saying to one who is financially destitute, "You have the freedom to spend money."

You may have been conditioned to believe that love is a commodity that is given and received, and you may feel that you haven't received much love. You may live in a love-starved darkness, searching everywhere for love, waiting for people to turn you on with love, blaming people and conditions for turning you off, for making you angry. When you live at the circumference, this is the way it seems.

To be able to fill your longing for love, it is important to understand the true nature of love. There is a basic insight, which I call the unity principle: "Wherever God is at all the whole of God must be, and because God is omnipresent, the whole of God's love must be present at every point in space." Thus God is not to be contacted "out there" and influenced to convey His answer of life or substance or love from where He is to where you are. God is present in entirety at the point where you are. All that is needed is that you become conscious of God's allness.

Couple the unity principle with the scriptural assurance that God loves you with an everlasting love and you can only conclude that you are ever in the presence of an infinite and eternal love energy from which all things proceed. Love is a creative flow that emanates as naturally from the center of you as radiation emanates from uranium. So it is not the absence but the frustration of love that is the human dilemma.

From the concentric perspective (life is lived from within-outward) we see that love is not a commodity that we fall into or out of, or that is passed from one to another. We do not love because we are loved, and only if we are loved. We love because God first loved us, because God is love within us, a focus of love *being* us. Love always flows forth from within to the degree that we let it.

Let's relate this abstract realization to a concrete situation: To *get along* with people is not dependent as much on them as it is on your willingness to *go along* with the flow. This is why I often say that getting along with another person is only 2 percent what he or she is and says and does, and 98 percent how you react to what that individual is and says and does. The statistics may be somewhat exaggerated, but the point is that if you are willing to accept your responsibility, any relationship conflict can be resolved and healed by getting centered in your love flow. It takes two to make a quarrel, but it takes only one to bring it to an end.

There is a dynamic activity of harmony and love everywhere, whether or not you are aware of it. This is what the "omnipresence of God" means. It is always present at the inmost center within you as a potential for transcendent power. The need is simply to give way to love's flow.

You may wonder, how do you lose the consciousness of this ever-present flow? You may never know. But one thing is sure, if you are being pushed around, you are out of it. You may want to fight back or cry foul. You may be absolutely certain that the problem is out there, in the motivations or actions of others. But your desire to retaliate or incriminate is a state of *your* consciousness. It evidences that, at least in that moment, you are out of the flow.

Jesus says, "Love your enemies and pray for those who persecute you, so that you may be sons" (Mt. 5:44-45). In other words, stop resisting and start loving. You may say, "I just can't do that. I have really tried to love them, but it is too much for me." But you see, to *try* to love is not to love. Love is not trying; it is *being*. It is not condescension or creating a facade of acceptance. It is letting go and giving way to the concentric flow.

Jesus was a master psychologist. He says that a man's enemies will be those of his own household. The important key to dealing with enemies is the awareness that they exist as enemies by reason of your enmity. If your enemies are completely out there, you have a difficult problem. You must defeat them or evade them. But if they exist within your mind as a feeling of enmity, then you have control. You can alter your thoughts, dissolve your enmity, and the enemy is routed as far as you are concerned.

Let's consider a down-to-earth illustration. Suppose you are standing on a street corner, waiting for the traffic light to change, when a truck or bus comes roaring by you right through a huge puddle, splashing you from head to foot. Telling about it you say, "I was really steamed. I mean, anyone would be angry." Let's face it, your reaction is easy to justify. You might even complicate it by saying, "And I had just come from a Truth lecture, engrossed in beautiful thoughts of love. What is a person to do?"

It is a difficult lesson, but an important one, to admit that your sudden flare-up of anger evidenced that beneath the facade of composure there was chaos within you at the time. You were disturbed by what happened because you were "disturbable." You were engrossed in thinking about love, how great it is, how it can change your life. But you were dealing with the four-letter word l-o-v-e. Love is not thinking about it; it is doing it. It is *loving*. Can you begin to see that if you had really been in a more loving consciousness, you would have dealt with the experience in an entirely different way?

There is an even more difficult self-admission: Because you were out of the consciousness of the flow, you may well have attracted the experience to you in the first place. This may be why, if you take careful stock of your habitual thoughts, a kind of paranoia might be revealed: "Everywhere I go I keep running into things like this." It is consciousness "outforming" itself.

If you understand the importance of keeping yourself in the consciousness of the concentric flow of love, you will see the problem with someone in the light of what it reveals about you. In other words, not, "Why did he do that?" but, "Why did I react as I did?"

If you remember that life is a matter of personal growth, then you will realize that your behavior in the face of the situation that occurred indicated a red-light warning of a crisis of consciousness. Difficult as it may be to see yourself actually doing it, you should be grateful to the person for showing you that you have an important inner adjustment to make. You might not want to make a display of it or people would think you had lost a few marbles, but if you find yourself exploding with anger or irritation over something another person has done to you, you should (figuratively) bow low before him and say, "Thank you for showing me that I have been sitting on a time bomb of inner chaos. Now I can do something about it." Of course we are being facetious, but not entirely. Think about it!

Listen to the words of Henry Drummond: "Life is full of opportunities for learning love. . . . The world is not a playground; it is a schoolroom. Life is not a holiday but an education. And the one eternal lesson for all of us is how better we can love."

One man pointed out that he is now grateful that his business has forced him to work with a particular associate, one whom he couldn't stomach, because it taught him a great lesson in living through loving. He says that when he finally realized that he couldn't change the situation, he decided to change his own thoughts. Then, through a concentric perspective of love, letting the all-sufficient love-flow go forth from him, he found that he not only began to get along with the man in their official relationship, but in time they became the very best of friends.

It is common for people to unrealistically expect the world to provide them with the kind of peace and love that can come only from within themselves. We may all tend to do this to a degree. We do not take people as they are, but as fits or misfits of our standards and expectations of what they should be or do. Then we either reject them outright, or we try to make them over.

This gives rise to the erroneous idea of "making friends." Sometimes a friend is one who agrees with you, or one whom you have converted to your way, and the friendship lasts as long as that individual remains converted. In truth you can never really *make* a friend. You can only *accept* a friend, and you can only do this when you are conscious of the concentric process of love that flows endlessly through you, limited only by your willingness to let it flow.

It is probably true that each of us will have to give up some long-held prejudices to understand this thing called love. For by nature every person is generous and loving, though you may have frustrated this impulse in endlessly subtle ways. It is not that love is absent, but that it is being frustrated. You are always *in* love, and love is always *in* you. This may appear not to be true when there is conflict between people, or when there is jealousy or suspicion. But whatever the situation, love is always present, for God is present, and God is an all-sufficient, ever-available flow of transcendent love.

In times of great crisis, when people are thrown together in the common bond of fear or insecurity, as in war, earthquakes, or blackouts, the subject of conversation is often how loving and mutually helpful people suddenly become. There is no logical explanation for the phenomenon other than that people really are this way inside, beneath the facade of their own faulty self-esteem.

But no matter what a person is or is not, no matter what he or she has done or left undone, everyone hungers to project love to the world. The individual may not and probably does not understand the working of love, that God always loves each of us, and is love within us, that we are created in and of love, and thus that we always have enough love to meet any situation. He or she may even tear at the world like a child tearing at a rag doll. But our urge for love and for loving is always present as an explanation for our hungers and drives, and also as a key to our potential for growth and achievement.

It is not easy to give up prejudices. You may say that you are surrounded by people with whom you have little or nothing in common, people who may seem to be beneath you, people who even resist your efforts to get along. You may wonder why you are there, in your job, or your neighborhood, or even in a family into which you have come through a relationship such as marriage. But you are there, and wherever you are God is — love is. Give way and let love flow. You may have your feelings hurt, you may be angry, resistant, resentful. But the result is that your flow of love is being blocked by your ego. Let go, give way to a stream of forgiveness and compassion. Suddenly you will know, as did Jesus of His malefactors, "They know not what they do."

You may say, "But how can I love these people? I don't even like them." But you see, to love is not an intensive of the verb "to like." Of course there are some people you do not like. It is almost visceral, as you may dislike certain foods or have particular tastes for colors. You may not be able to help what you like, but you can help what you love. Love is a willingness to let God's love flow forth through you in the direction of your involvement. But the marvel is, if you say yes to love in the direction of some person you don't like, often something happens to cause that person to become a friend. It is probably true that some of the most beautiful relationships in our lives never happen, simply because we do not exercise the freedom to love, thus releasing the possibility of true communion.

It is not easy to change a lifetime of conditioning to the

idea that love is simply something that goes on between two special people, to give way to the larger perspective of love as a harmonizing power between all people. We may hunger for a love relationship with one person, all the while frustrating the flow of love in our relationships with life.

Giving way to love is nonresistance. For most people nonresistance is a vague theory practiced by people like Gandhi and Martin Luther King, or a willingness to get stepped on and pushed around. Buddha touched on a theme that is found in various forms through the writings of all the great mystics of the ages: "The man who foolishly does me wrong, I will return to him the protection of my most ungrudging love . . . and the more evil comes from him, the more good shall go from me."

This is not easy, for it goes against the grain of all our normal reactions to life. Most of us have a compulsion to straighten people out, to give them a piece of our minds (which is to give up our peace of mind), and to "get even" when we have been hurt. But the only way we can ever get even with another is to love, bless, and forgive him or her. If we don't, we will become slaves.

The French philosopher Montaigne lived during one of the most tumultuous periods of modern times, in sixteenth-century France. He was a lover of peace who hated wars, and who pitied the soldiers and civilians who were its victims. His lovely château in southern France stood unharmed in the midst of several battles, despite the fact that he was an aristocrat and the chateaus of aristocracy were all being thoroughly plundered. His home was a lighthouse of love and peace. While battles raged around him, soldiers on both sides left the place intact, even stopping in for rest and refreshment. Montaigne saw the experience as a challenge to keep peaceful in the midst of turmoil. While meeting it with nonresistance, he felt he was effectively destroying his enemies, thus settling war. Without a doubt Montaigne was the first articulate pacifist.

Society often pressures us into taking a stand for or against something. A good citizen gets involved, we are told. What do you think about the missile crisis, about abortion, about capital punishment, or about many other ideas currently in the news? I suggest a better way: Take a stand for unity. It is not being indecisive or disinterested. It is, rather, taking a concentric perspective, letting the flow of love go forth to enfold and bless every person and every issue involved.

Edwin Markham gives a formula that may appear to be simplistic, but which is actually a dynamic credo for dealing with problem people:

> He drew a circle that shut me out,
> heretic rebel, a thing to flout,
> But love and I had the wit to win,
> We drew a circle that took him in.

In your imagination, draw a circle of love around all people and groups of people about whom you are concerned. Become an arbiter of peace. Bless all people, relationships, organizations, or nations with whom you may be in any way involved. Meditate long upon the idea that you are a channel for the expression of the divine flow of love. Feel that love going out to bless all who are in the purview of your interest or involvement.

Every day before setting out into your world, prepare yourself by getting the realization of the concentric flow of love. Make a commitment that you will give way to love in every situation. In this love-flow you will see and respond to the divine in all people. Instead of expecting the world and the people in it to make your day happy or harmonious, you will establish yourself in the kind of consciousness that you desire to experience, letting it flow through you and go forth from you.

Recently I received a card from an anonymous radio listener. Its simple message was, "Just to say I love you." On the inside, "Happy Valentine's Day." What a lovely surprise! I could feel the exuberance of this unknown person who had become a conscious channel for the expression of great love. Holidays like Valentine's Day are lovely times for sentimentally remembering certain people with hearts and flowers. Such times can also be sad times of emptiness for those who are lonely and friendless. But it is all too easy to designate only one special day for a love commitment to important relationships. It might be helpful to observe instead an occasional "great week of loving," a time of special discipline to keep in the flow of love and to maintain a loveful consciousness in all relationships.

It can be an important inventory week, taking stock of all the people or groups of people who evoke emotions of love and affection and friendliness, or on the other hand of hatred and resentment and distaste. The former need your love like a family needs succor. The latter are an important insight into the causes of any inharmony or confusion or illness in your life. Meditate on love, not just as a relationship to fall into, but as a dynamic flow of the universe into you. See this love going forth to encircle all people and take them in. Spend a few minutes every day getting centered in the concentric flow of love. It will turn your whole life around. You will probably decide to make every day a great day of loving.

You can never be fully alive nor get the most out of any day if you are engaging in resentment, bitterness, or downright hatred. It is a terrible burden to dislike people, even to be critical. It is so much easier to love people concentrically, to be patient with them, even to forgive their errant ways.

People may have shut you out, nations and ideologies may have erected barriers, but in this age, we must have the wit to draw a larger circle of love to include and bless all people and groups of people.

Remember, divine love is present in its entirety at every point in space at the same time. So all the love in the universe is present in you. No matter what the experience, there is always enough love to go around. At the "still point" within you there is a veritable fountain of healing, prospering, protecting love energy, potentially ready and divinely willing, instantly and constantly, to solve, resolve, and dissolve any human problem.

If you are surrounded by any kind of conflict, dissolve your concern in a love meditation. Then draw a circle around the whole scene. Thus, all parties, all sides, will come into your sanctuary of consciousness. Here you can overwhelm them all with love to heal all conflict, and open the way to understanding communication. It has been said, and if you work with this concentric process you will come to agree, that love is the greatest thing in the world.

SIX

THE ART OF
GIVING YOURSELF AWAY

Take a few minutes to reflect on the symbol we have suggested to explain concentrics. It is extremely simple, but the awareness it reveals is profound. In the margin of the book, or in a notebook, if you prefer, draw two intersecting lines that form two cones touching at the points, indicating the inmost center where Being is in the process of being you. In the cone at the left write the words, *infinite creativity;* and in the cone at the right put the words, *being your potential for success and creative achievement.*

We have said that life may be experienced in many ways and on various levels of consciousness. But it can only be lived from within-outward. All life, all substance, all creativity flow forth from within. This is concentrics.

Life is a giving process, and the great need is to learn to consciously give way to the inner flow. Instead of being preoccupied with how to get from the world, we need to learn how to stop blocking the flow of the divine process within.

It is my feeling that there has been an overemphasis in metaphysical studies on what I call "the success syndrome"—getting there at all costs, demonstrating more money and better jobs. The focus tends to be on how to get more from life by prayer and treatment. I feel that there is often a gross materialization of a beautiful spiritual Truth. I have discussed this at length in my book *Spiritual Economics: The Prosperity Process.*

Why do you work? I recall one of those amusing radio shows featuring Fannie Bryce as "Baby Snooks."

Snooks says, "Daddy, come play with me."

Daddy replies, "I can't dear; I am working."

Snooks asks, "Why do you work, Daddy?"

"To earn money."

"Why do you want to earn money?"

"So that I can feed you."

And Snooks says, "Daddy, come play with me. I'm not hungry."

You may smile at the question, Why do you work? for it seems perfectly obvious that everyone works to make a living. But if this is the only reason you can come up with, it is one of the errors that must be unlearned. You spend a large portion of your life engaged in some kind of gainful employment. Thus, if your attitudes about work in general and your job in particular are not correct, then truly you are working against yourself. You may seek diligently to achieve prosperity and success, but unless you unlearn your error thoughts, you will forever be out of sync with the creative flow of the universe.

A German educator, Friedrich Froebel, had a refreshingly positive sense of the concentric process at work in the individual. It would be a fine thing if his idea of work could be stressed in our contemporary educational system, or at least through parental training at home. Froebel's thoughts are that the delusive idea that we work for the sake of preserving our bodies and procuring bread, houses, and clothes is degrading and not to be encouraged. The true origin of our activity and creativeness, Froebel believes, lies in our increasing impulse to embody outside ourselves the divine and spiritual element within us.

You can have no finer explanation of concentrics in relationship to your work.

I want to suggest to you a change of perspective that will seem much simpler than it really is. I want you to begin to think of your work as a giving process. Jesus suggests a simple beginning: "Do not let your left hand know what your right hand is doing" (Mt. 6:3). In other words, don't get trapped in the error of equating what you earn with the work you do. How common it is, and yet how mistaken, to be influenced by the another-day-another-dollar syndrome. Let your work, whatever it may involve, be an outworking of the creative flow, engaged in through the sheer joy of fulfilling your divine nature. You will prosper, and you should do so; but it will not be because you have made money in your job. The work in the job is the means by which you build a consciousness of giving, which in turn gives rise to an outworking or receiving flow. It is a subtle distinction, but an extremely important one. If the left hand (receiving your pay) knows what the right hand does (the work of your job), then there is no real giving, only bartering. It is selling your soul for a mess of pottage. All the elements needed to fulfill the prosperity law for you are missing.

The new word in modern analysis of what ails our economy is *competitiveness*. We are told that the international balance of payments is out of balance. Products are manufactured abroad and then exported and sold in this country cheaper than we can produce them here. Of course this causes many layoffs in the American work force. So the current dilemma is how to make us competitive again. The economists always come back to the matter of productivity. The focus is normally on equipment and technology. However, there is something much more basic and more personal. It is overlooked because of the paranoid feeling that "the world is picking on us."

It is what I call "The Great Depression of Worker Attitudes." Something tragic has happened in America in the period since World War II. It is a steady erosion of the old-fashioned work ethic, leading to a loss of the sense of work being done in the context of the whole person. It would be impossible to estimate the effect that this has on the productivity of American industry and the stability of the economy.

In any metropolitan area we can see great masses of people going off each day to work that is perceived as drudgery, and which becomes an empty and meaningless process of putting in time. So often work is thought of as a necessary evil, a life sentence from which one may ultimately retire as time off for good behavior. We talk of entering the labor market as if we sell ourselves in exchange for the wherewithal to exist. It is not uncommon to hear a person describe his job with a shrug, "Oh, it's a living!" But if this is the attitude, then it is not a living at all. It is little more than a drab existence giving rise to all sorts of physical, financial, and emotional problems.

It always saddens me to see people working for a paycheck for which they do as little as they can. It is sad because I know the law under which the person is building hidden frustrations for which he or she must in time pay the price. The person may think one can get away with slipshod work, fudging on time sheets, and calling in sick to get the day off. An individual may well get away *with* it. But no one can ever get away *from* it. For it exists in consciousness, and eventually the piper will have to be paid.

When we understand the concentric perspective, we realize that life is a process of living from within-outward. Thus, fulfillment in life can come only through giving, not through getting. You may say, "But I always do all that I am expected to do." But do you always expect enough of yourself? Do you do all that you *can* do? If an individual does less than the very best possible, he or she might be the one who is shortchanged. That individual could be storing up what some might call "bad karma."

Some time ago one of my "research assistants" (people who voluntarily send me articles, stories, and quotations clipped from magazines and newspapers) sent me an editorial from *The New York Times*, "in case you missed it," which, strangely, I had. The editorial talked about the new generation of people ages twenty to thirty moving into the job market, and the deficiency of any sense of work ethic in many of them. A personnel manager refers to them as "benefit bums" (which I find a little harsh). He says that during interviews these people hardly listen to the duties of a job being explained. They ask about salary, vacations, sick days, and other benefits. They shop employers for benefits. That, to them, seems to be the essence of employment. They are quite ready to take, not to give. Once hired, the syndrome continues. They are chronically late in the mornings; they take the longest coffee breaks and lunch hours, and they start getting ready to leave a half hour before quitting time. Their skills are usually low, their motivation even lower. Further, the editorial continues, they seem to suffer from strange maladies such as "Monday affliction" and "Friday afternoon paralysis." They may be the product of the spreading "welfare psychosis" that has afflicted countless families in the past generation. They seem to say to their employers, "Pay me because I am here, not for what I can do."

Let me not be misunderstood. Let's be realistic. Of course there will be benefits in every work, and there should be. But the new perspective that every student of Truth should reach for reveals and gives way to the "benefits of an orderly universe." Jesus said it simply, "As you give so will you receive." But in this phrase there is a key word that points to the concentric process. It is the word *as*. Even in the very act of giving, there is receiving. It is like the water faucet that receives a continuous supply of water while the water runs freely from the tap. Thus the most important benefits from your work are the creativity and substance that flow forth from within even *as* you work.

When young people begin thinking about career goals, they may ask a parent or career counselor, "What is a good field to get into?" We should answer, "Do you mean what is a good field, or what is a good field for you?" Then they will likely ask, "But what field will pay the most money?" The wise adult will respond, "That is a pressure you should resist as long as you can. In the long run the work that will prosper you the greatest is the work you can put yourself into with the most enthusiasm. If you take that which offers the greatest immediate return, you may well frustrate your own potential, even your eventual earning power." The young person may persist, "But shouldn't I try to find a job with a future?" It is an opportune moment to teach a great Truth: "That is a delusion. In a way there is no future in any job. The future is in you. When you find your right place, you will release that which makes for a good and happy and successful future."

Emerson certainly reflects the concentric perspective when he says, "No matter what your work, let it be your own. No matter what your occupation, let what you are doing be organic. Let it be in your bones. In this way you will open the door by which the affluence of heaven and earth shall stream into you."

What a beautiful insight, revealing prosperity as a divine flow from within. When you work in the right consciousness, when your work becomes organically a part of your whole self, and when you do your work out of that commitment, no matter what other people do, no matter what the compensation may be, when you do it for the health of your own soul, then you open the way for the affluence of the universe to stream into your life.

It is a beautiful realization. But how quickly we forget, rushing off to work in the morning, reading the morning paper over a cup of coffee, and then plunging into a meaningless job, which offers little more than degrees of boredom throughout the day. If this is the attitude, then it follows that there will be a problem of financial stringency in one's life. It will do little good to run frantically to a spiritual counselor, asking prosperity prayers. As the Quakers say, "When you pray move your feet." In this case, move your hands. Stir up the receiving flow by giving.

One of the airlines used a slogan successfully for many

years: "We have to earn our wings every day." Yes, and you have to earn the level of consciousness by which you are sustained and prospered, every day. You may say, "Oh, I have been on this job for years, and I know the work so well that I could do it with my eyes closed." But what is happening to you as a person? You must earn your wings, not to please your employer, but for your own spiritual well-being. What you do in your work every day may not affect your salary (at least immediately), but it vitally affects your focus of consciousness, which regulates the flow of affluence into your life.

Try a little experiment. For one week, take some time every morning, before you commence doing what you do, to say, "I am going to earn my wings today." It will be simply a few moments of commitment. Then begin your work in the awareness that there is a creative process flowing through you as you work, making what you do much more creative, and leading to greater success and achievement.

In his classic work, *The Prophet*, Kahlil Gibran says: "When you work you fulfill a part of earth's furthest dream, assigned to you when that dream was born, and in keeping yourself with labour, you are in truth loving life, and to love life through labour, is to be intimate with life's inmost secret."

"Life's inmost secret" is the divine pattern in you, which you can really know only when you are giving yourself in service. You can work for money and prestige and climb to the pinnacle of success, and still not know yourself, thus seeking other avenues of escape such as alcohol and various other dependencies and addictions. All this because your work doesn't satisfy you. The reason is that you are not satisfied or fulfilled in yourself.

However, when you are intimate with life's secret, your work becomes your calling. The word *vocation* comes from the Latin *voco*, meaning "I call." Begin thinking of your work as a calling. The creative process is calling, singing its song in you and as you. The work becomes easy and fulfilling, and you become prosperous and successful in it. There is no pressure, for "the affluence of heaven and earth" streams into you.

Get involved in what is sometimes called "possibility thinking." It is possible for every person to be a success in work. The only one who can keep you from succeeding is you, by blocking your own creative flow.

You are not a helpless creature adrift on the seas of life, trying desperately to make something of yourself against impossible odds. The creative intention is vitally involved in you. Thus, your very desire to get ahead, the urge to succeed, is your intuitive awareness of something in you that wants to succeed through you.

Get the concentric perspective of the universal creative process rushing, streaming, and pouring into you from all sides while you do your work. Feel this so strongly that your whole being bubbles with enthusiasm and your fingers virtually tingle with power. Work in this consciousness, and you will be dynamically in the flow of life. You will be constantly giving yourself away. Because the law is as you give so you will receive, there will be a fulfilling demonstration of receiving.

It would be helpful to take an inventory of your work experience. Do you go to work with a sense of eagerness in the morning? Is your work a happy experience and your place of work a place in which you enjoy being? If not, then you are probably extremely tired toward the latter part of the day and exhausted every evening when you get home. You may think it is because of the amount of work you do, but it is more likely the result of your resistance and resentment.

You may feel unappreciated in your work, underpaid and overworked. These things may be true. But your life is lived from within-outward. No matter what conditions prevail in your place of work, what happens to you and in you is the result of your own consciousness. Alter your thoughts, and your fatigue will leave. Bless your work. The word *bless* means "to confer honor upon." Give yourself a raise (in consciousness). Raise your thoughts about your work, your associates, your employer. I once read an article entitled, "Why Not Give Your Boss a Raise?" This deals with attitudes. Bless all things related to your work — people, conditions, finances, opportunities. Commit yourself to a disciplined positive attitude about them.

You may say, "But I don't like my job. I feel that it is beneath me." There is no high work or low work. If your work is essential to anyone, it is ennobling to perform it. It may not be your true place (the ideal place that you may ultimately achieve). But it is your right place, the place in which you can do the growing you need in order to progress to the greater unfoldment of your good, to experience the better possibilities of life for you. Don't indulge in the fantasy of finding more interesting work. There is no "interesting work," only interesting people doing their work in an interesting way.

A girl took a job in a grocery store to earn money for college, but she soon found that she was earning only enough to live on with nothing to save. She hated the work, feeling it was beneath her. But the fact was, due to resistance and a lack of motivation, she was a poor clerk. One day the bookkeeper left, and the boss indicated that she might take the job. But, alas, she had to face up to the fact that she was totally unprepared for anything better. It was a shock, both humbling and revealing. So she took stock of herself and made a commitment to begin thinking more of giving and less of getting. She started arranging the items displayed in the store in a more artistic way. Her boss noticed. He put her in charge of display. She discovered that she had a real talent. She enrolled in night school, taking some courses in the specialized field. She took some other display jobs after hours. Eventually, she took a position with a large display company where she is now an executive. When she changed her attitude and began to grow in her job, when she began to think "give," a whole new world opened up for her.

You may say, "But I am unemployed. How can I think of giving myself away?" Many people who are unemployed unfortunately have become unemployed not because they lack skills, but because they lack a sense of giving. They may hunger for the opportunity to get on a payroll somewhere, but their whole attitude is one of getting (getting a job so they can get money to live). But you see, employers are not in the welfare business. They may even be sympathetic to your plight, but they rarely let their business sense be ruled by emotion. They are looking for someone who can help them do their work. Begin to think give! Let it show in your manner and your words. Instead of finding work, your greater need is to find yourself. Change your self-image from "one who is unemployed" to "one who is ready for work," eager to serve, to give yourself away. We are dealing with universal law, not caprice. Thus you will draw to yourself or be drawn toward the kind of work opportunities where you can be blessed and be a blessing.

One of the key ideas in the Bible is to wait on the Lord. It is a much misunderstood command. The word *wait* comes from the Hebrew word *gavah*, which means to "bind together." Thus to wait on the Lord means to integrate yourself in consciousness with the power and potential of the divine creative process within you. Paradoxical to the normal connotation of sitting and waiting for something to happen, waiting on the Lord is an attitude that implies go, do, work.

Before undertaking any project, wait on the Lord by taking a moment to go within and experience oneness with the creative process at the "still point." It is an important moment when starting out to seek employment or when commencing work for the day, a time to get a sense of the concentric flow. It is a letting go of the human perception of compensation dangling before your eyes. Your work will be love made visible. You will feel the inner urge to give yourself away, to do all you can do to the utmost of your skill.

There isn't a job in the world that can't be done better than it is being done. No one is doing right by his employer or by himself if he simply rocks along, going through the routine motions of doing his work. Make a continually renewed commitment to give way to life by affirming: *I will do what I do better and better and better, and I will do more and more of what I do.*

I would like to reflect for a moment or two on the closing lines in the chapter "The Work of Your Life" in my book, *Life Is for Loving,* changing from the first person plural to the first person singular to personalize the thoughts.

"I will go off to work in the morning with the eagerness of the lover going to meet his beloved, and I will engage in my work in the kind of mutual sharing that lovers experience together. I will return from work at the close of the day with the joyous feeling that I have given much of myself to my work and have received much from my work. But in the giving and receiving, the greatest joy will be in knowing that I am in tune with what Gibran calls, 'life's procession that marches in majesty and proud submission towards the infinite.' "

SEVEN

FROM WILL
TO WILLINGNESS

One of the great statements of the Bible is found in the book of Isaiah, "To us a son is given . . . and his name will be called 'Wonderful Counselor' " (Is. 9:6). We have been led to believe that this referred to Jesus. It is a mistake common to orthodoxy that tends to obscure the dynamics of biblical truth. The new insight in Truth reveals that Isaiah is referring to the divine depth *in* Jesus, which is also the divine depth in you. There is a son-of-God self in you, and you must call it "wonderful."

This is to say that you are a unique individualization of God. You are unique and different and wonderful—full of wonder. It is this very wonder that Truth is all about—discovering it, identifying with it, and releasing its inner splendor. An important implication of Isaiah's "wonder" is that life is lived from within-outward. Until we achieve this concentric perspective, we live at the circumference of life, and we try to generate in the human that which can only flow forth from the divine. To achieve any kind of effectiveness in life, we must act from conscious awareness of our innate divinity.

Most success conditioning courses emphasize the need to develop a strong will. They stress that much failure in life is due to a weak will. People who do not have the will and determination to know what they want and to go after it rarely succeed. One success course states this graphically: "Smash the wall that blocks your path by the projection of your will."

It is probably true that there is a shortage of will in many of us. We have been conditioned to a life-style where the will has had little place. Things have been done for us; security has been carefully provided. Many parents have felt that their role was to break the will of their children so that they would be obedient and well-adjusted. It may be that one problem of the welfare state is too much security, which softens the will to achieve self-reliance.

The will is an important driving force in our lives. To progress in life we must develop a sense of determination and persistence, the ability to keep on keeping on when things seem to stand against us. This is very important! But the will needs to mature into willingness, a conscious process of letting go. Otherwise, the will tends to become willfulness, stubbornness, battering down doors to achieve personal goals. In other words, there must be awareness of that which works in us and willingness to let it unfold.

In his letter to the Philippians, Paul says, "For God is at work in you, both to will and to work for his good pleasure" (Phil. 2:13). This statement, along with many other references to the will of God, confuses many people. For many have grown up with the teaching that sometimes God wills suffering and limitation. This is undoubtedly why many people say or at least think to themselves, "I am not ready to get involved with the church yet. I'm not ready to have God telling me what I must do. I want to do my own thing for awhile, to enjoy life. Eventually, after I've had my fling, I'll go back to church and (with a pious sigh) let God's will be done."

This comes from an erroneous concept that God has a mind separate from yours and mine, and that, out of some capricious intent, God may will something contradictory to the desires of our hearts. It is important to wake up to the realization that the will of God could never intend for us anything other than that which is highest and best.

What is God's will in nature? It is for the seed to germinate and grow and bear fruit and flowers. It is the natural flow of the life process. The will of God is exactly the same for you and me. Of course, with us there is a matter of consciousness that comes into play. Still, the will of God is the ceaseless longing of the Creator to perfect Himself in that which is created.

In "The Lord's Prayer," Jesus affirms, "Thy kingdom come, Thy will be done, on earth as it is in heaven" (Mt. 6:10). This kingdom is the within of you, the divine flow in you, the wholeness of mind, of love, of life, of creativity in you. Let it come, let the creative intention be done. Let it be outformed in your life, even as it is involved in Divine Mind.

The will of God for you is life. God's will can never be for death. Orthodox preachers become terribly upsetting to their flock when they should be comforting. They talk of sickness as "God's visitation," and in funeral services they drone, "God has taken his little one home. It is not for us to question. God's will be done." This is a total misapprehension of the nature of God, the creative process of the universe. Jesus clearly said, "It is not the will of my Father who is in heaven that one of these little ones should perish" (Mt. 18:14). God cannot be life-giving and death-dealing at the same time.

God is life, and life seeks only to reproduce itself in life. God's will is always for health and healing. It is the upward pull of universal life seeking to vitally outform itself. It is Being seeking to *be you*.

The study of Truth constantly emphasizes mind. We are told, "All is mind; mind is the great power; through mind we can do all things." But it is important to realize that this refers not to your mind, but to Divine Mind. There is a sense in which we could say that we do not have minds. We have brains that are highly sophisticated organs through which minds work. But what you may call your mind is really your consciousness of and within Divine Mind. Consciousness is the pivotal point in the whole study of Truth. The concentric perspective reveals that the whole of infinite Mind, eternal life, boundless love, and divine substance, are present within us, and it is God's will that they flow forth *as* us in a personal experience of abundant life. The only restriction or limitation is our consciousness. Healing, success, fulfillment in love are achieved through expansion of consciousness.

It is important to practice focusing your perspective until you can see yourself in the context of the whole. It does not come easily. A discipline is involved. There is little question that in a completely human perspective, you are at the mercy of the conditions at the circumference of life.

("I of myself can do nothing.") However, through your oneness with the allness of infinite Mind, you can do all things. You can realize all things if you can let go of the will of the human (which may well be willfulness) and turn from will to willingness. Let the infinite-mind process work through you.

When you are unaware of this concentric perspective, you may try to make things happen through your use of mind by trying to program the mind with a lot of affirmative statements. When you talk about *making* a demonstration, you may very well be thinking of making things happen by force of will. If so, there is likely to be much frustration and disillusionment in the process.

At some time in your life you have undoubtedly blurted out, "I just don't understand. I tried my very best, but it simply hasn't worked out." The truth is, you have never really tried your best unless you have let go of the frantic attempt to achieve at the surface and let the concentric process unfold.

The word *try* is an anemic term, not really suitable for use by the sincere student of Truth. From its etymological roots the word implies a random selection or culling out of good and bad potentials. There is no faith in an inner focus implied at all. Sometimes we say, facetiously, "I gave it the old college try." But that old college try "won some, lost some, and some were rained out." Not a very impressive motivation. When you *try* to do things (clenched fists), you are working from the outside-in. When you let God do them through you, you are working from inside-out (concentrically), and success must result.

This is not to say that you should not make an effort. Work to be done calls for a determined will and the hands with which to do it. But it is remembering, "I of myself can do nothing," and yet being in tune with the wonder power, "I can do all things."

The primary example of the letting go process is the story of creation as found in Genesis. We have been blinded to the Truth by viewing the allegory in an anthropomorphic sense. If you read the creation story in Genesis 1, you will see that even in this brief résumé of a long and complex process, the emphasis is not on *trying* or even on *making*, but on *letting*. The real miracle was the imminence of the creative process in which there could be no strain or drain. "God said, 'Let there be light . . . . Let the dry land appear . . . .' " (Gen. 1:3, 9). God didn't try to make a world. God said, "Let!" to every act of creation, and it was so. No strain, no sweat, no depletion.

Paul says, "Have this mind among yourselves, which is yours in Christ Jesus" (Phil. 2:5). This is significant. There is no way that you can *will* God-Mind to be in you. The fact is that you live and move and have your being in infinite Mind. There is no way that you can get more of infinite Mind in you, for infinite Mind is present in its entirety at every point in space. There was no more of infinite Mind in Jesus, or in Buddha, or in Shakespeare, or in Einstein than there is present in you this moment and every moment of your life. Isn't that exciting?

Paul is talking about consciousness. We need to develop a great consciousness of infinite Mind. I make a statement often that succeeds in shocking some people. I say "succeeds" because it is intended to disturb. It is my feeling that we need to be challenged to let go old concepts and press forward in Truth. The statement is, "There is absolutely no difference between Jesus and you and me in terms of how we were created and how we live within the all-potential Mind of the Infinite." Of course there is a world of difference in our awareness, our self-perceptions; in short, in consciousness. For instance, you are equal to your neighbor in that you both live and move and have being in the same universal flow. But there may be a vast difference between you in the way you think and feel, the way you give way to the creative process.

Our need is to develop the quality of consciousness that Jesus developed. How do we do this? By autosuggestion or mind programming? By affirming words of Truth repetitiously? We may *try* to renew the mind by trying to make it over in this manner. But all we wind up with is the memory of a lot of words, a mind glutted with metaphysical clichés.

Again, the key is to let. Your mind is a consciousness of infinite Mind. It *is*, not *can* be if you work night and day at the task. You *are* the Christ, not *may be* at some future millenium. See it in this light: The tulip bulb is a tulip even when it is nothing but a dry and shriveled bulb. The egg is a bird. The acorn is an oak tree. You are a perfect expression of God. Of course this refers to an ultimate. The finished work does not require a great will to make it, but the willingness to let it unfold.

There is much confusion concerning persistence in prayer and "letting go." Between the power of the will and the need for willingness. We may be told to keep on and keep on keeping on, to resist the temptation to stop short or to give up. We may be reminded of the fable of the man cracking the great stone by persistent blows on the same spot. However, what we need is not persistent willfulness but persistent willingness, a persistent attitude of letting go.

There is a common misunderstanding of the prayer process. Prayer is one of those things that we often try to do. There may be a belief that prayer changes things, yet when conditions seem mountainous and difficult, we may pray "hard" about them. But hard prayers, frantic prayers, pleading prayers are self-limiting prayers. Prayer is not the means of getting an answer. It is giving way to the answering flow. It doesn't make the answer. It simply accepts the answer. We are told, "Before they call I will answer" (Is. 65:24).

The key to effective prayer and treatment is to pray believing that you have already received, and to remember that it is the Father's good pleasure to flow forth as the healing, or employment opportunity, or overcoming, or harmonious settlement of a relationship problem. It is already a part of the divine will. So your efforts to pray are amiss if you are trying to make God do the work, to *make* a demonstration. It might be more appropriate to begin using the phrase, *let* a demonstration.

It is interesting that when we may have been pushing, straining, persistently treating, and unconsciously pleading about some problem or need, when discouragement sets in, we say in resignation, "Oh, I give up!" In that moment there may be a giving way and the dawning of a new attitude of willingness. Often a dramatic change takes place. There may be a marvelous unfoldment of the healing or happy outworking. When we move from will to willingness, things begin to happen.

It is my strong feeling that not enough attention is given in the teaching of Truth to the need to let go the human ego and its willful insistence and persistence in demonstrating things. There is often the attitude, "I know what I want and when I want it, and I know that in Truth I can have it." Thus there is a perception in which God becomes a genie, hopping to your command.

There are those who say, "Know what you want. Create

a master plan, and pray persistently for it." Fine. But what we rarely understand is that human perception does not always see far enough ahead. So we do not always know what is best for us, even what we really want ultimately to do or be. Unconsciously we tend either to sit with folded hands, doing nothing, or we get on the horse and ride off in all directions. We may well be willfully working for that which, in our deeper awareness, we do not want. We may feel that we should want it, or that it is the thing that is being done. But we need to let go and let our divine self lead us, to listen to the voice of Prometheus.

There is a classic story of the woman who wrote to Silent Unity for help in getting a particular man to marry her. She became a frequent correspondent, always asking Silent Unity's prayer help for this hoped-for marriage. There was a lull in the letters, and it was assumed that her problem was solved. Then came another letter from this woman, now asking prayer help in getting rid of the man.

Remember, the great formula of divine creation is "Let there be"—not "There must be," or "Dear Lord, make there be," but "Let there be!" No suggestion of strain, hurry, anxiety, or doubt. The goal is a willingness to let go of human strings and personal desire. Problems exist only in human consciousness, not in God or the dimension of our own God-self. The need is to get yourself out of the way and lie low in the divine circuits. Stop trying to force a condition into or out of the body temple. Relax, and in receptivity to the everywhere-present life of Spirit, let health take possession of you. This requires much faith and discipline, and the practice to achieve that discipline is where will comes in—the will to let the divine will be done.

Get it into your consciousness that what you desire, God desires for you. That which you work for is seeking you.

Stop trying to make money; let substance flow. Stop trying to make a healing demonstration; let health and life have their way in you. Let there be! This is the prayer that never fails.

Remember the concentric process: Life is a within-outward flow. Take time at the beginning of every day to let go and get in tune with the flow of your good.

Many people are good achievers but poor receivers. They set goals of achievement of things and positions in the world, but they do not look within for support. Thus they do not receive the means to keep on achieving. If you commence any project, thinking only of what you must try to do, you will come up short. Thus it will always be, unless you pause to let go and let the creative flow have its way in you, through you, and as you.

Remember, prayer does not make answers; it simply accepts answers. In prayer, we need to relax the involuntary tension of the mind and let the transcendent life and substance flow. It is not as much something to do as it is to let be done. Give way to life!

An important preparation for prayer is relaxation. If you are eager to demonstrate, anxious over some challenge, look to your hands. Are your fists clenched, palms moist, muscles taut? Then you are involved in will and willfulness. This is not prayer. Turn from willfulness to willingness, from persistence to letting go.

EIGHT

THE ART
OF RECEIVING

Life for unaware people is a purely horizontal experience. Such people go from experience to experience, like a water strider skittering across a pond. In this consciousness, life is purely a matter of what happens around or to an individual. But when the Truth dawns in consciousness, individuals become aware that they are spiritual beings with a vertical dimension of experience. They begin to see that life is lived from within-outward, and that all life, all substance, all creativity flow forth from within.

In this chapter we want to consider a side of the giving process that is often overlooked. It seems obvious that behind every act of giving there must be willingness to receive. We have referred to the water faucet as an illustration. When the faucet is turned on, it is giving. There must be a source and a pipeline that is open and receptive. In order to receive water from the faucet, there must be a giving as well as a giving way.

We live in an opulent universe. The prodigality of nature is revealed in the beauty of the flowers, in the abundance of harvesttime, and in the dynamic energy that is generated by such a wonder as the Niagara River in its drop over the Falls. Look closely at this illustration. At Niagara, though the energy is limitless, we can have only as much energy as we accept through the great turbines. Note carefully that the great generators that harness the power of Niagara Falls are not creating electricity. They are the technological means through which we have learned how to receive the energy that is already there. In a phenomenon such as a power blackout, which plays such havoc with a society dependent on electricity, there is no lack of power. The problem is in the acceptance of power, blocked by a problem in the stations that lose their receivership. When the faulty circuit is corrected, the energy flows, and we can have all that we will accept and use.

I refer often to Jesus' parable of the prodigal son. This is an important parable, for it contains the whole theology of the Bible in a nutshell. It is a capsule of Jesus' teaching. It is a great idea which can lead us to freedom and overcoming when we unlock its secret message. You know the story. A father has two sons. The younger son comes to his father and asks for his inheritance, which the father gives to him. The son goes out into what is called "the far country," where he squanders his fortune in riotous living. Eventually he is impoverished, reduced to feeding pigs for a farmer. In that culture this is a symbol of hitting the absolute bottom of the economic ladder.

However, you have to hand it to him; it became a time of soul-searching and growth. The Bible says, "He began to be in want" (Lk. 15:14). He realized that even the servants in his father's house had more than he had, which means that he woke up from the dream-sleep of separation and remembered that his true inheritance was in the inner kingdom, that "still point" where the allness of God becomes the eachness of the individual. It is one of the great discoveries of life when we realize that life is lived from within-outward. So the means whereby he could experience abundant life was forever present within him. So he said to himself, "I will arise and go to my father" (Lk. 15:18). This indicated a period of discipline and overcoming. Though the outline of the story skips over the months of work, sweat, and tears involved in the growth that took place in his "coming to himself," it is important to recognize that this change didn't just happen in a stroke of good fortune. When the young son returned home, he was a much different person than the one who had gone out. He had lost the prodigal and servant consciousness. When the father showered him with blessings, putting a robe on his shoulders and a ring on his finger, and gave him a celebration feast, it was not a father pampering a spoiled brat. It represents consciousness outforming itself. He had worked his way home and earned a new dimension of inheritance.

There is another facet of the story that is rarely told. It concerns the older brother. He did not go out and live riotously; he did not squander his inheritance. He stayed home, worked hard in the fields, and was completely faithful to his father. Now we can see the older son looking on at the festivities over the return of his wayward brother, green with envy and consumed with jealousy and bitterness over the grave injustice. He is thinking: Look, I did not run off and live an orgy of irresponsibility and waywardness. I stayed home and worked, and slaved, and accepted my responsibility. How come no one has ever given a feast for me? So he comes to his father with his complaint. The father says to him, "Son, thou art ever with me and all that I have is thine." The truth is that we all live within infinite Mind. We can have all that we can receive. This refers to consciousness, the sense of personal "worth-ship."

The older son was living in the midst of the abundance that was now being showered on the young son, who had regained his worthiness. But the older son did not have the consciousness to receive it. Examine this story carefully and you will see that the older son was really a prodigal at heart. He was in the same state of consciousness the prodigal was in when he went out into the far country. But the older son lacked the nerve to do it. His jealousy indicated his feeling of self-reproach for his lack of the discipline to develop his own awareness of oneness.

There are times when we, too, may be jealous of others, wondering why they get the breaks. Perhaps there is an office party celebrating a co-worker's promotion. You may wonder why you didn't receive the promotion so that the party would be for you. But the law is: All that is mine is thine. You live within the infinite mind of God, and you always receive or achieve in your life that which you can receive in consciousness. In other words, that of which you feel worthy.

It is always sad to witness an experience where a person has been hungering for prosperity and advancement in a work situation, and then when an opportunity arises, he or she is overwhelmed and unable to fill the job. Even though the individual involved may have been praying diligently for the increase, in fact that person wasn't ready for it. There is a matter of preparation through education and training. The person may either have to pass up the opportunity or take a job that proves unmanageable. In either case it is an embarrassing situation.

The problem may be that the person does not feel worthy of or attuned in consciousness to personal desires. Thus, there exists an inability to receive. For truly, success is not getting there but earning the right in consciousness to be there.

You may test your receivership and discover how well and how graciously you receive. Just imagine that someone makes an unexpected gift to you. It may be someone in your office, or a neighbor, or a friend. It may be an offer to assist you when you are in a bind, to buy your lunch when you left your wallet at home. Imagine how you might feel, what response you might make. Would you accept the gift or the offer graciously? Or do you see yourself protesting, "Oh, no, I can't let you do that!" Or if you do accept it, would you then hurry to reciprocate?

This inability to receive graciously is the evidence of a spiritual problem that may answer many questions about other phases of your life, such as, "Why do I not get ahead?" "Why do some people get all the breaks?" Or, like the elder son, "Why do I not rate a banquet?"

Some years ago I had been working with a man who was struggling with alcoholism, with modest success. It was a Memorial Day weekend, and the man offered, out of gratitude for my spiritual help, to come to my home and work in the yard. I felt it might be good therapy for him, so I agreed. He put in a long, hard day, trimming overgrown hedges, mowing the lawn, and weeding the flower beds. He literally transformed my garden. I can remember the joy showing on his face. No doubt something wonderful was happening to him as he was gaining a feeling of self-respect. He came to the door and thanked me for letting him do this work.

Perhaps no one is completely free from the tendency to be a poor receiver. In this case it is probably a rationalization. Out of gratitude for the fine work the man had done, and thinking that because he was not working and could certainly use the money, I pressed a bill into his hand. I don't recall the denomination. It might have been more than I should have offered him. I will never forget the look on his face. Almost instantly the look of joy faded, and he assumed a look of defeat. It was as if I had kicked the props out from under him, which I really had. I watched helplessly as he walked down the street with an obviously heavy heart. I found out later that he had gone to the nearest bar, commencing a three-week binge.

This was a great lesson to me, one that I have remembered painfully over the years. I was chagrined, for I had the very best intentions. But there is no getting around it—I failed him. I insisted on putting his beautiful gift, which was his reach for self-respect and decency, on a purely commercial basis. Thus I actually rejected his gift. It was a difficult lesson.

As a follow-up, I am happy to report that in this case I had a second chance, in that I later resumed some counseling work with the man. I am happy to say that he did eventually conquer his alcohol problem. Also, because we discussed at length the whole experience, it was possible for him to learn the importance of receiving, too.

Receiving is a vital aspect of giving way to life. Many

people delude themselves into believing that they are generous givers, when in reality they may be extremely selfish, for they withhold from others the joy of giving. The classic example is the "check-grabber." When you are enjoying a meal or light refreshment in a restaurant with some friends, this person always arranges to get the bill so he or she can have the ego fulfillment of playing host. One important kind of receiving is giving other persons the opportunity to give.

Back in the times when trains were the normal means of travel, they usually had a rear car that was called the "observation car." I recall that as a child I always wanted to go out on the platform and watch the landscape whiz by. I had a history of getting some words confused, so I might say, "Daddy, let's go back and ride the obligation car!" How many of us ride the "obligation" car through life? We fear being under obligation to people, especially if it is someone we don't know. There is probably a poor self-image involved, a sense of unworthiness to receive, thus unwillingness to accept something without reciprocation.

If it were not so serious, it would be funny to see the ridiculous struggle between people to "get even" in the matter of giving. You have us over to your house for dinner, and we must immediately make plans to have you over to our house for dinner. We hop on the obligation car.

Consider the Christmas card syndrome. You may go over your list thoroughly to be sure that you have sent a card to everyone who sent you one last year. Then you receive a card the day before Christmas from someone not on your list. Do you dash out and buy a card to send so you will not be on the obligation car? Subtly, it is a way to cancel out the gift. Why can't we be big enough and generous enough to give the person the opportunity to give?

We may pray for help in a situation, and when someone comes forth "out of the blue" and offers to help, we say, "Oh, I can't let you do that!" Why not? How do you suppose the answer to prayer will come? Through a magic manifestation from the sky? We are told, "Every good endowment and every perfect gift is from above, coming down from the Father of lights" (Jas. 1:17). God is the giver and the gift itself. So when our good comes, no matter how, we must learn to give thanks to God as the source, and then bless the channel through which it comes.

Under divine law, when I have a need to receive, someone else has a need to give. So even as I may have been blessed with the answer to my prayers when someone offered me something, he or she got the answer to a prayer in a subconscious motivation to give. Thus, if I refuse to accept a gift, or even if I accept it grudgingly with a sense of obligation, I cut off my own good and hold back the other person's good too.

If you have been having difficulty helping someone, let that person do something for you. Let him or her give in some way. It may seem humbling, because it is you who may want to help the other person. But giving may be the very thing that particular individual needs to regain self-respect and self-confidence. You may give the most by giving way to the other person's gesture of giving, by being a gracious receiver.

Humans are naturally attractive creatures—drawing people, ideas, and conditions to them. However, we tend to interfere with the process by our hang-ups in consciousness, such as a poor self-image, or feelings of guilt and unworthiness. If something comes to you, even if accepting it may be a humbling experience, be a gracious receiver. Affirm: *No one comes unto me but the Father sends him.* It is the divinity of you that has created the attraction.

It can be a test of consciousness. One way to pass the test and take a step in growth is to accept the gift, and then work on your thoughts to expand self-realization. But if you reject the gift, you not only completely reject the overture of the other person, which is that individual's opportunity to grow through giving, but you also fail to pass the test of growth in yourself, because something in your consciousness is seeking to outform itself, and you are refusing to let it happen.

John says, "But to all who received him . . . he gave power to become children of God" (Jn. 1:12). We are all spiritual beings, rich and creative and wonderful. But we have the right to experience this only if we are willing to receive, to let God or the channel of God bless us with increase.

All that comes to you is an opportunity for growth, and you take the step in growth when you accept graciously. It is true in all phases of life. But nowhere is it quite as true as in the consciousness of receptivity to the divine flow.

Prayer is an experience in receptivity. It is important to realize this, for so often in treatment of working to demonstrate through prayer, the emphasis is on getting. There may be an attitude of trying to get God to do this or that for us. The plain truth is that there is nothing you can get God to do for you that is not already done in God-consciousness. God is not the "Big Man" who sits out there waiting for you to come hat-in-hand, begging, pleading, supplicating, waiting for you to "pass the test" so He will do something for you. Note how the Bible articulates the principle: "Behold, he who keeps Israel will neither slumber nor sleep" (Ps. 121:4); "I have loved you with an everlasting love" (Jer. 31:3); "It is your Father's good pleasure to give you the kingdom" (Lk. 12:32). In God there is a constant givingness, as constant as the water supply in the faucet. Thus, when you turn on the tap, you don't have to beg the well or the reservoir for water. There is pressure, and the water automatically flows. So prayer is not trying to get God to give. It is a matter of learning to receive.

"Why doesn't God answer my prayer?" This is the wrong question. It should be, "What in me keeps me from accepting that which God so freely offers?" Jesus said, "Come, O blessed of my Father, inherit the kingdom prepared for you from the foundation of the world" (Mt. 25:34). The purpose of prayer is not to try to get God to give, but to resolve in our consciousness the attitudes that may be blocking the spontaneous creative flow. Not, why is life rejecting me? But, why am I failing to accept the abundant life that is being freely offered to me?

In this book we are dealing with the importance of developing a giving consciousness. We hope that you will dedicate yourself to a new giving attitude. Think give, and you will get! The other side of the coin is: For all giving there must be receiving. When things begin to unfold for you, and blessings come, be a gracious receiver. Certainly bless the giver. But give thanks to God. Dedicate yourself to the giving consciousness. However, remember that an important part of giving is "giving way." Accept your good as the demonstration of the law—the receiving or "come-back" of previous giving. Then let your giving start a new chain.

NINE

THE SCIENCE OF GIVING

In a time when there is so much emphasis on acquisition as the key to fulfillment, interestingly, there is also a widespread sense of meaninglessness. It is surprising how many persons moan, "My life has no meaning!" Such an attitude leads to boredom and depression, and to various kinds of dependency and addiction.

Life's meaning is not to be found out there in relationships or jobs or baubles. Life is something one releases from within. It is purely concentric. When you know who you are with an awareness of life flowing forth abundantly through you, then you put meaning into your work, give meaning to experiences, and derive meaning from relationships by the giving attitude in which you meet them.

How important is the need to alter the tendency toward dealing with life as an exterior acquisition, rather than as an interior unfoldment. What is called for is a very simple and basic orientation: Think "give" instead of "get"!

Giving has become so completely identified with church collections and pledges and with pious acts of philanthropy that it is difficult to think of the word without referring to what is often called "the commercial of the church." The emphasis is normally on what the gift is *to*, and what rewards come back in the form of "heavenly grace," a name on the stained-glass window, and a healthy deduction on the income tax return.

Our culture has to teach the science of giving. Religious institutions have failed people through preoccupation with their own needs to receive support—the new roof on the church or the foreign missions project. The needs are often very real and urgent. But the responsibility to teach people how to live by giving goes by the boards.

Preachers have talked of returning a portion of one's income to God, which skirts the issue by dealing with an anemic God of the skies, who bargains with us for a giving return. The activity of God, like the water in the faucet, is a giving flow. There is no way that you can turn it back unto itself. The creative flow, again like water in the faucet, ceaselessly longs to flow forth. True giving is giving way, letting God's kingdom come, God's will be done in earth as it is in heaven. It is letting God use you as a channel to pour forth. The exciting thing is that, as yours truly has proven over a period of forty years in the ministry, a religious institution can achieve an abundance and to spare to meet all needs, without church budgets, and fund-raising drives, and pulpit appeals for funds.

Now certainly, an effective church is worthy of the

faithful support of its congregation; but fundamental to that effectiveness is helping people to understand the principle of giving. It is not enough to prod people to give *to* something, for it can become completely perfunctory. Every person needs to know what he or she is giving *from,* and thus to consciously give way to the divine flow.

The law is: As you give so will you receive. The key is in the word *as.* You are receiving from within even while you give. Thus the giving is receiving, giving way to the Great Giver. The giving of the Infinite is constant. However, its flow is dependent upon our will to give way. We see, then, that to sustain the flow of good, it is necessary to get into a giving consciousness.

In the study of Truth, it is important to know that giving is rooted in the cosmic law of causation: "Give and you will receive." One of the important first steps in the practice of Truth is to learn how to give. This commitment is imperative to the well-balanced life.

Become a good giver. Don't delude yourself. Keep your channels open through commitment to some kind of systematic giving. When you get into a giving pattern, things in your life will change dramatically, and you will experience such a sense of meaning and fulfillment in living that you will wonder how you could have lived so long in any other way.

A logical question at this point is, "But to what or to whom should I give?" We all receive so many appeals from religious and charitable organizations pleading for support. First of all, get the firm attitude of giving. Make a commitment that you will become a giving person. When you get the consciousness of giving as the basic motivation in your life, along with it will come the desire as well as the guidance as to how you give, where you give, and what you give. It will come naturally. The important thing is not what you give *to*, but a clear understanding of what you give *from*.

There are two distinct kinds of giving: (1) Giving that is *outer-centered*. (2) Giving that is *inner-centered* (concentric).

Outer-centered giving depletes the giver, while inner-centered giving endows the gift with that which transcends its intrinsic value. It so blesses the giver that, like a faucet filling the cup, the giver is immediately and correspondingly filled from within.

If you see a need and, out of a sense of duty or sympathy, give to that need, the giving is outer-centered. On the other hand, if when you see a need, you turn to the realization of the all-sufficiency of God and then give, not just to the need but from the consciousness of divine supply, then your giving is inner-centered or concentric. It is a subtle distinction, but knowing this process and acting on it is one of the most important insights to effective living.

When giving is outer-centered it is a personal thing. The ego is very much involved. There is a need to be seen and appreciated. If there is no appreciation, the giver is likely to feel hurt, to cry, "Such ingratitude!" When the giving is inner-centered, it is impersonal. The emphasis is not on the gift or to whom or what it is given, but on the inner source of love and substance from which it is given. The act of giving means a giving way to the flow that springs forth from the wellspring of all-sufficiency. There is no sense of depletion in the giving, for the giving is also receiving. Because the act is finished in the giving, there is no expectation of reward or appreciation. If there is an expression of appreciation, it is simply an added blessing.

Outer-centered giving is most often withheld because of

a sense of personal inadequacy, postponed until that nebulous future when things will be different. "When I get the raise in salary," or "when the children are out on their own, then I will begin to tithe or do things for the church," and so forth.

Inner-centered giving is a spontaneous flow that uses any and all means as channels. It is giving of what is available now, but the gift is maximized by the love and gratitude that flow forth from within.

When we understand the "science of giving," we realize that there is a wellspring of life, substance, and intelligence within us, for we are, after all, individualized offspring of an affluent universe. Ours is the privilege at any time of giving way to the universal flow. This leads to an important revelation: If there is ever lack of any kind, something is blocking the flow. The most effective remedy? Give!

I refer often to my mother, for she was a great influence in my life. What she gave me was not an intellectual perception of deep metaphysics, but a simple awareness of basic Truth principles, and a never-to-be-forgotten demonstration of living by faith. She was also a minister-teacher of the new insight in Truth.

Mother was a great blessing to many persons, mostly on a one-to-one basis in counseling. She had an interesting approach. No matter what else she did for people (she was a good teacher, and so they were enriched with a practical understanding of Truth), she always insisted that before they left the session they make a commitment to some form of giving. This was during the depression years in the early thirties, and many of her counselees were unemployed and financially strapped. She would stress the Truth that if they wanted help or healing, they had to open the channel by giving way. She would say, "Just sit there with your eyes closed and examine your life. What can you do that will fulfill your desperate need to give? If you can't give money, do you have some unneeded clothes you can share with someone in need? Or can you see how you can give more of yourself in your work, or (if unemployed) volunteer your services somewhere? But don't leave this room until you can see yourself initiating the giving process." Of course they might leave a "thank you offering" to her for her prayer support. Or they might make a contribution to her church. They might go forth with a planned intention to start a giving process by some form of largess.

To mother there was no equivocation in the matter of "As you give, so will you receive." The emphasis was strongly on the little word as. As you give, in the very move to give, you open the way to the inner flow. She always said, "Your giving is your receiving. The process begins right now, if you do."

Get the idea firmly fixed in mind that you are always in the presence of infinite and eternal energy from which all things proceed. Thus it is never for lack of life or substance or love that you experience difficulties, but because you are out of the consciousness of the flow. One of the most effective ways to get back into the flow is through giving. If you have been thinking lack, thinking of the need to get, you must now think "give."

When you understand the importance of giving, you may look for ways to give. There may be times when you cannot find the help you need, but there is never a time when you cannot give way to the inner flow and be the source of help for someone else. It is in giving that you establish your legitimate need and thus open the way to receive.

Paul says, "And my God will supply every need of yours according to his riches" (Phil. 4:19). It is a fantastic promise! Note, however, that it does not say God will supply your lack. A need is a vessel ready to receive. Lack is like a cup turned upside down. There is no capacity to receive. It is not that God turns His back on you refusing to assist you. For the law is: It is (always) the Father's good pleasure to give you the kingdom. There is a divine desire to meet every need of your life in relationships, in employment, in physical wholeness, and in your financial affairs.

To find the abundant life that Jesus promises when you get the awareness of Truth, it is important to make giving a fundamental part of your life, which calls for some form of systematic giving, such as tithing. This normally involves giving one-tenth of your income to a church or religious institution, preferably to wherever you may be receiving your spiritual help. The choice is yours to make.

Let me say first that tithing is an excellent practice, which I strongly recommend to anyone who is seeking to change his or her life and to experience stability in health and abundance. However, let us look at the practice beyond the superficial and materialistic way it is normally approached. Tithing is normally encouraged for all the wrong reasons. Some of the claims made and arguments set forth make the tithing concept a gross materialization of a beautiful spiritual truth.

The practice of tithing is normally supported by many quotations from the Old Testament of the Bible. Under Levitical law, the tithe was a form of tax that was required of the Hebrews. It wasn't a love offering or charitable contribution at all. In a religious form of government, a theocracy, tithing has often been the method of creating revenues to support the government. Most often quoted as the authority are Malachi's poetic words, "Bring the full tithes into the storehouse, that there may be food in my house" (Mal. 3:10). It was like the Internal Revenue Service saying, "Pay your taxes so we'll have money to run the government."

It is significant to note that Jesus makes only two references to tithing, and in both instances it is referred to as a practice of someone who is being criticized. For instance, in one of Jesus' tirades against the Pharisees, He said, "Woe to you, scribes and Pharisees, hypocrites! for you tithe mint and dill and cummin, and have neglected the weightier matters of the law, justice and mercy and faith" (Mt. 23:23).

Jesus did not teach tithing, as such. But He specifically emphasized the law of giving. Jesus said, "Give, and it will be given to you; good measure, pressed down, shaken together, running over, will be put into your lap. For the measure you give will be the measure you get back" (Lk. 6:38).

In Old Testament times tithing was an enforced discipline, laid down for people who did not have the spiritual development to work with divine law. It took its place alongside hundreds of laws and observances governing everything from sanitation to meditation. As training wheels on a bicycle may help a youngster to learn to ride unaided, so all these laws were right and appropriate for the people of that day. This is not to say that you and I may not benefit by "training wheels" in many aspects of our sociological and spiritual development. Certainly the practice of tithing is an excellent training process, a fine means of engaging in systematic giving. You may read scores of testimonials of persons who have gotten themselves on the road to a giving consciousness, and who have demonstrated health and prosperity through the disciplined practice of tithing. This is commendable and wonderful to hear.

However, tithing is often presented as a divine law rather than as a training discipline by which to work toward knowledge of the law of giving. Sometimes it is said that tithing is a "magic cure" for all ills. But there is no magic whatever in tithing. If some great demonstration results, it has come through fulfilling the law of "as you give, so will you receive."

Bicycle riding is based on the law of balance, working with the law of inertia. The training wheels have nothing to do with the laws by which the bicycle is propelled. They simply help the rider to experience the working of the law. Why do I insist on this distinction? Because tithing is not an end, but a helpful means toward the end of living totally in a giving consciousness.

You see, the materialistic way in which tithing is often presented is misleading. We read such things as, "Tithe your way to riches." But to tithe as a kind of good investment, expecting to get back more than one gives, is not truly giving. It is a kind of bartering, a selfish attempt to work the law instead of letting the law work you.

Those who get into the tithe-your-way-to-riches consciousness are building their houses on sand. With dollar signs in their eyes, they are more concerned with what they are giving *to* than what they are giving *from*. But this need not be the case. It is a matter of motivation. The question is, "Do I tithe to get things, or to get a greater awareness of divine law? Do I analyze the effectiveness of my tithing on the basis of my income or my general well-being?"

Now let's not misunderstand this point. Giving is a fundamental spiritual law. You cannot live without giving, as you cannot live without breathing. You inhale and you exhale, on and on, constantly. It is a part of the vital process of life. But there is no rule that says you must inhale so many cubic inches of air. It depends on your lung capacity. Now it may be that you are not breathing efficiently, so a specialist might give you some breathing exercises to help you restore your balance. In the same sense, tithing can be an excellent program to help you become established in the giving-receiving rhythm.

The principle is: In any complication you may experience in life, the most effective road to overcoming is through giving. However, tithing is not necessarily the way to a giving consciousness. It is possible that you may neglect the consciousness of giving while you are enthralled with the "magic" of tithing. Also, you may fall into a rut of methodically, even painfully, writing the tithe check every month.

Here is an example: A person desires success and prosperity in his or her work. This individual has been convinced that tithing will work its magic. After several months of tithing, when nothing shows signs of changing, this particular person becomes discouraged. The feeling is that through tithing the "dues have been paid," so a promotion or raise in salary should come through. Yet if you analyze job performance, it is quite obvious that he or she does not give much to work, and consequently is not very effective. This person may frequently arrive late and talks to co-workers incessantly during the day. But this individual feels that by tithing things will change. The employer in this situation could say, "There is a raise in salary for you, which will become effective *when you do.*" A person can tithe but not give. Tithing *can* be a way of getting into a giving consciousness, but it is no substitute for a giving attitude and a giving performance.

The great need is to give way to the divine flow, and tithing can be an excellent means of achieving the giving consciousness. However, the giving must involve something more than the writing of a tithe check. Malachi refers to "the whole tithe." This means all of you, not just all of your money. When Jesus criticized the Pharisees for tithing without love, He could have been implying that they tithed decimally and not spiritually.

"Prove me now," challenges Malachi. Prove the law in action. This involves going the second mile in meeting obligations, turning the other cheek in relationships, and forgiving "until seventy times seven." It means diligence in keeping the high watch of positive thinking and loving reactions in overcoming the world of tribulations. In other words, life is consciousness, so it is foolhardy to suppose that the law can be fulfilled by anything less than a total and broad commitment to achieving a high-level consciousness.

Jesus emphasized giving as the way to achieve this degree of consciousness. Give and you will receive. Think give, and you will receive. Think of your work as giving. Think of every relationship as an opportunity to give. Give to your children, give to your neighbor, give to passersby on the street. Think give. Give way. This is to apply the concept of concentrics. Life is lived from within-outward.

As a part of this commitment to the giving consciousness, give of your substance, graciously, wisely, and without thought of return. Think not of what you are giving to, for that can turn the mind to condescension or "giving to be seen of men." Rather, think of what you are giving from, and thus feel humble in realizing that you are simply giving way to the divine flow.

Now certainly, tithing is a helpful and practical plan for getting order and system into your giving commitment. It makes as much sense as keeping a budget, and it can be given appropriate recognition in the budget. But it is wise to remind yourself that the 10 percent is simply a disciplined reminder to bring the whole tithe. There is nothing magical about 10 percent. It could be twenty or fifty. The important thing is that the giving consciousness must continue where the tithe check leaves off.

If you sincerely desire to grow and ultimately dispense with the "training wheels," a good plan is to use the tithing slide rule as a means of checking up on your spontaneous giving during the year. Instead of following the regular ritual of writing a tithe check, work for a commitment to give way to the divine flow on a sustained basis. Just let yourself be free as a joyous giver with no thought of contracts or bargains or great benefits of success. Take pride in the growing maturity you demonstrate through the year by giving the whole tithe. Then, at the end of the year, when you are engaged in an audit of your fiscal year for tax purposes, total up your giving and see how close you actually come to a 10 percent giving performance. What a tremendous feeling of fulfillment you will experience when you find that your giving exceeds the tithe. Now it could be said that you have "put away childish things." For the "whole tithe" now means no tithe, in the sense of obligation. Now you are joyously in the flow of life through your giving consciousness, for you are essentially a giving creature, and life is lived from within-outward. On human levels of consciousness you may emphasize getting and having as the prime goals; in spiritual consciousness, seek the way of *giving* and *being*.

Reference is often made to the law of tithing. But tithing

is not a law. It is a technique for fulfilling the law of giving. There is no magic in it, any more than there is magic in the flow of water when the faucet is turned on. There is no need for magic when you work diligently to keep in the flow of life.

Tithing is a powerful technique to employ in order to achieve the discipline of spontaneous giving. Ultimately you will never know if you are a giver of the whole tithe unless you test yourself by putting away the tithing practice for a period (even one month may be a good test). This may be difficult for you if you are strongly conditioned to the decimal way of giving. It is like a child learning to ride his bicycle with training wheels, and then continuing to use the trainers all his life. It is unlikely that the child will ever know if he could ride steadily without them.

The important thing is to get into a giving consciousness and let your hands give way to some kind of giving flow. A disciplined program of tithing may be a giant step in spiritual growth. But don't stop there. Dare to take the step beyond tithing, so that in spontaneous giving, rather than stringently giving under pressure, you achieve or exceed the tithe. People who achieve this consciousness are ready to step forward into a new age.

TEN

THE ULTIMATE GIFT

Philosophers of every age have declared that a person has only to know himself or herself, to discover the secrets of the universe. This is the true purpose of the Bible: to help you to know yourself. Of course, this is not at all the way it has been taught. It has been represented as teaching about God, the absentee landlord of the universe, who does certain things for some inscrutable reason known only to Him. Thus, you may study the Bible all your life, and you may be able to quote the Scriptures at every hand, and still not know yourself. You may believe in God, but a god who is totally irrelevant to life.

The Bible has great meaning, but not in a literal sense or even in a historical sense. For most if not all of it is allegorical. In a personally symbolic sense it is the story of one person—you! Everything in it—names, places, and events—symbolizes stages of consciousness in the evolution of the person, of you. All the stories of the Old Testament, when considered symbolically, begin to unravel like a mystery story when metaphysically interpreted.

The final stage of the spiritual evolution as symbolically outlined through the Bible is depicted in the characterization of Jesus Christ. This is not to doubt the historicity of the story, but it is to indicate that the story did not survive the long years by reason of its historical truth alone. It has survived because it dealt with the Gospel Truth, the message of Jesus, and the metaphysical import of His life.

The word *gospel* comes from the Anglo-Saxon root which means "god-spell." This has the connotation of good news or glad tidings. The word has great relevance in your life and mine today, for it deals with that ascending urge basic to all people since Adam. It is the upward pull of the infinite creative process within each of us—a force that explains Jesus, but that also encourages us. Unfortunately, this is not how the Gospels have been presented. The "good news" has usually meant the idea that God has seen fit to forgive humankind for its hopeless sins, to clothe Himself for a time as a person in Jesus, and to offer Himself as a living sacrifice to atone for our misdeeds. It is what I call the "hideous dogma of the vicarious atonement."

Once we catch the ideal of the ascending urge in us as symbolized through the whole Bible, we see Jesus not as God becoming a person, but as a person becoming God, a person feeling the pull of the divine within himself, and through discipline and great overcoming, going all the way to what Teilhard calls the "omega point." That Jesus did it is good news, for it means that it is a reachable goal, a repeatable demonstration. Didn't He say, "All that I do you can do too"?

The central point of "good news" of the Gospel story is not really Jesus, but the Christ spirit that He expressed and the universal principles He taught and demonstrated. The good news is not that Jesus was divine, but that every person is inherently divine, and that each individual contains within himself or herself the wherewithal to surpass self, and that it will never be given to any of us to reach that which cannot possibly be surpassed.

As we come to the conclusion of this study, would you have imagined that we could present a whole book about giving without subtly or directly laying out all kinds of projects for you to give to, along with stirring appeals to do so? We hope that you have by now gleaned the message that we are not concerned with philanthropy or charity or even church giving except as recipients of a giving flow that results from the awareness that life is a giving process. Unless and until you learn to give way to life, you cannot experience life in its fullness. Money giving, important as it is, is a small part of the wide spectrum of the giving process and practice in the life of the spiritually mature person.

We have been using the word *concentrics* as descriptive of life flowing forth from within. Actually, we might be more explicit if we referred to what we call metaphysics as "concentrics." The word *metaphysics* was coined by Aristotle to describe the next logical step up in the study of life and the universe. The prevailing philosophy of his time was *physika*, the science of life. So his next step was "metaphysika," the science of life and that which transcends physical life. Walt Whitman summed it up when he said, "Man's not all included between his hat and his boots." This is an important fundamental study of humanity today.

The problem is that it is possible to create an elaborate cosmology, the idea of the omnipresence of God, the imminence of God-Mind, and the innate divinity of humanity, and still fail to get it all together. We may still deal with duality, even if it is a kind of metaphysical duality. God is still "out there" or even "in here." But as I say in my book, *Discover the Power Within You*, "God is not in you like a raisin is in a bun, but like the ocean is in a wave." The wave is never more nor less than the ocean expressing as a wave. You are never more nor less than God expressing as you. This is true oneness! Much prayer, even some metaphysical treatment, is two-ness. It is still dealing with God as separate from yourself, still trying to contact God, trying to get His attention, trying to earn His favor and support.

The psalmist said, "Be still, and know that I am God" (Ps. 46:10). This means to let go and let all the self-limiting identifications be dissolved, and know yourself as God expressing as you.

Recall how we use the word *concentric* in referring to circles or spheres one within another, all having a common center. Reflect again on the image of an ever-widening series of circles all emanating from you at the center. Thus, wherever you are or whatever you may be involved in, you can never get outside the circle of which you are the center. The key to effectiveness in the resolution of conflict is to return to the center. This reveals why a centering time of meditation or inner prayer is the key to the prayer for help in solving problems.

How important it is to get the perception of God, not as the being of the skies to whom you appeal for help, but as omnipresent, or, if you will, omni-centered. The whole of God is present in His entirety at every point in space. At the point where you are, you are the self-livingness of God. In a very real sense, you are the self-givingness of God.

As I have said again and again throughout this book, there is no understanding life without realizing that it is a giving process. All life, all love, all substance, all wisdom flow forth from within. You are a spiritual being, and life can only flow forth from within-outward.

There is a time every year when our consciousness of giving is put to a severe test: Christmas. There is much that is beautiful and magical in the Christmas season. But there is also a strong tendency to get caught up in what Philip Wylie calls, "the hopped-up, pressure-laden, status-seeking, competitive degradation of Christmas."

The problem for most persons is that Christmas traditions and family expectations pressure us to slavishly go through an annual charade of erecting the facade of Christmas like a Hollywood set. But the mistletoe and possibly the Christmas tree, too, are quite likely plastic. More and more the whole observance of this lovely holiday becomes perfunctory and superficial. Little wonder that a growing number of modern-day Scrooges cry out, "Bah, humbug!"

Christmas is for children, it is often said. Yes, and for the sleeping child that lies dormant within us.

Christmas chronicles the Nativity, the birth of Jesus in a manger those long years ago, the legend of the Wise Men following a star, and the shepherds in the field, and the angels that sang, "Glory to God in the highest." What child is there who could not tell this story? Yet, what adult is there who understands the personal symbolism that relates it to life in this time?

Whatever may be your perception of the greatest story ever told, one thing is certain: It is the story of the greatest gift ever given. "God so loved the world, that he gave his only begotten son, that whosoever believeth in him should not perish, but have everlasting life" (Jn. 3:16 A.V.).

How this has been misrepresented as saying that Jesus is God's only son, and that only by believing on Jesus can we be saved! But the great gift, truly the ultimate gift, is God incarnating Himself in and as a human being. Salvation comes by believing in this God self or Christ self within us.

A medieval mystic monk, in a day when he could have been burned at the stake for heresy, courageously said, "God never begot but one son, but the eternal is forever begetting the only begotten." This is the magic key that unlocks the mystery of John 3:16. The "only begotten" is that of you that is begotten only of God. You may be begotten of your parents hereditarily, and you may be begotten of your culture environmentally. You may also be begotten of your academic experience. But there is a you that is begotten only of God. God so loved the world that He gave you, or gave Himself in the form of you.

Christmas calls us to give birth to the Christ of our nature, symbolized by the Nativity of Jesus, born in the manger. We are so easily pressured into giving that is motivated by conformity, by obligation, by guilt, and by status, which drains our energy as well as our funds. Also, we drift into a "getting" consciousness and we pursue things of the world. Like the prodigal son in the far country of materiality, we come to know want. Christmas calls us to wake up, to come to ourselves, and to get back into a giving consciousness. This is so beautifully symbolized in Christmas giving—or it should be.

The poet says, "The gift without the giver is bare." Why?

Because when you simply give an item, it is something that depletes you in giving. When you give in the spirit of love and service, it is giving out of the overflow, and thus the gift conveys something far transcendent to its material worth. You are enriched in the giving, and the recipient is blessed in the receiving.

How often we are caught up in trying to find a gift for the person "who has everything." But of what avail is it to give the finest gift if you do not give the gift of yourself?

The ultimate gift to you is God's gift of the creative flow in which you are the image and may become the likeness of the whole being of God. When we really understand this process, we discover that true giving is at the same time a receiving, a giving way. For the ultimate gift is that in which there is no strain or drain, but there is actually an increase in the giving. It is one of the universe's mystic secrets. It is getting the concentric perspective in everything you do, in everything you give.

Now, let us consider this mystic process on a level where we can all identify with it. If I have one dollar and you have one dollar, and if I gave you my dollar, and you gave me your dollar, we would still each have only one dollar. But if I have an idea and you have an idea, and if I give you my idea, and you give me your idea, we would each have two ideas. This is the ultimate gift! Ideas, like seeds, multiply and grow. Even if I give the dollar, if I give it in the transcendent idea of abundance, there will be a multiplication, as when Jesus fed the multitude from five loaves and two fish.

When you catch the idea of God's ultimate gift of the Christ pattern and potential within you, and when you see that you are this ultimate gift of God, then you begin to understand Jesus' injunction to let your light shine, to reach out and let your life be as a preaching of the Gospel, as you become what you want to share. Edgar Guest once said in a poem, "I'd rather see a sermon than hear one any day."

One of the greatest ideas that has ever been articulated is that there is a God-sized person within the soul of every one of us. Paul says it in words that Charles Fillmore said were the most important message of the Bible: "Christ in you, the hope of glory" (Col. 1:27).

The fullest life is that which is committed to giving the gift of the Christ, the gift of your transcendent self, certainly at Christmas, but also in your work, in parenting, in tithes and offerings to the place where you receive your spiritual help, and in community service.

It is important to keep centered in the conviction that the kingdom of God is within you. The health you seek is within you. The substance that is the root of the prosperity you seek is within you. The love that you hunger for is within you. The golden road to receiving is in the kingdom of giving.

If I may be permitted to reiterate the closing comments of chapter one: "There is a new world awaiting you, a new level of life open to you, and a new experience of the dynamism of the Truth that you have been experiencing. Get the concentric perspective. Have an occasional meditation when you return in consciousness to the center. Realize that at the center within you the activity of God flows forth as you. Concentrically speaking, what you seek is seeking you. Discover the wonder of giving. It is the better way. The day will come when you will insist that it is the only way."

Give way to life!

Printed U.S.A.   6-1761-10M-11-89